JEAN CUNNINGHAME GR.
family with a strong Naval trac
contemporary of Admiral
Gibraltar during the Napoleon
of Wellington. From his bea
inherited in full measure the dash of spice and joie-de-vivre that is such
a strong Spanish characteristic.

Perhaps it was because of this that she enjoyed being always on the
move with her parents and her brother as a child. Her young life in the
1930's as a sailor's daughter meant birthday parties on board her
father's cruiser in South Africa, long journeys by P&O ships to the far
east, a spell in China at Canton when the town was being bombed by the
Japanese, and the subsequent bombing of her own home on the Clyde
in Scotland during the Second World War. She was also to experience
Hitler's flying bombs at the end of the War, living with her parents in
the Commodore's House in Chatham Barracks. Her proudest moment
came when she was invited by the First Lord of the Admiralty to watch
the great Victory Parade from the balcony of Admiralty House in
London the year after the end of the Second World War. She was just
eighteen.

Lady Polwarth lives with her husband, Lord Polwarth, in the Scottish
Borders, enjoying her large family, and helping with both local and
national charities, such as the R.N.L.I. (her grandfather, Commander
Charles Cunninghame Graham had been Deputy Chief Inspector of
Lifeboats in the 1880's). Music has continued to play a large role in her
life, and in the 1970's she was chairman of the Scottish Baroque
Ensemble, and also of St. Mary's Music School in Edinburgh. In
Scotland, in the 1980's, she started up Yehudi Menuhin's highly
successful international scheme for young musicians "Live Music
Now".

# Sailor's Daughter
## 1928–1946

JEAN CUNNINGHAME GRAHAM

*Prefaces by*

**RICHARD HOUGH**
(Biographer and Naval Historian)

*and*

**ADMIRAL SIR JULIAN OSWALD, G.C.B.**
(First Sea Lord 1989–1993)

"One foot in sea, and one on shore, . . .
Then sigh not so, but let them go,
And be you blithe and bonny."

*Much Ado About Nothing*
William Shakespeare

Distributor: Shelwing Ltd.
127 Sandgate Road, Folkestone, Kent CT20 2BL
Tel: (0303) 850501   Fax: (0303) 850162

First Published 1993
Reprinted 1994

Published by
Lady Polwarth, Easter Harden, Hawick TD9 7LP

© Copyright 1993          ISBN 0 9522632 0 3

Printed and bound by
Buccleuch Printers Ltd., Hawick, Scotland

*For my grandchildren* ...

Sophie, Ellie, Anna and Jake Jauncey
Jeremy and Thomas Jauncey
and, last but not least, Angus Maudslay
born September 1993, 100 years after my father,
Admiral Sir Angus Cunninghame Graham.

# PREFACE

I have enjoyed this book enormously, it is just what it should be: a rather tender reflection of a child's character, and at the same time a radiant reflection of the times and circumstances of her life. *Sailor's Daughter* tells us what it was like to be just that. Her father, Admiral Sir Angus Cunninghame Graham, would have been proud and admiring of it.

RICHARD HOUGH, London, *August 1993*

My father spent his life in the Royal Navy, from the age of 13, and so have I. It is therefore inevitable that I should have picked up from him much of his love, understanding and loyalty to the service. He especially valued his friendships, many of them made by chance of an appointment, and kept for life. Few, if any, of his colleagues he more admired than Jean Cunninghame Graham's father. Angus Cunninghame Graham was the Captain of H.M.S. *Kent*, an outstandingly happy and successful ship engaged in the hazardous and unpleasant Russian Convoys at a most difficult period of the Second World War. My father, the Commander, enormously liked and respected his Captain, from whom the whole ship took its tone. This respect and friendship lasted for the rest of their lives. I am delighted to write this preface to pay tribute to Jean's father and to my own father – two great officers and gentlemen.

JULIAN OSWALD, Hampshire, *August 1993*

# ACKNOWLEDGEMENTS

THE ENCOURAGEMENT I have been given to write down my memoirs of a particularly exciting childhood has come entirely from my children. I hope the book will prove to be a sequel to my father's own memoirs, *Random Naval Recollections,* which has provided so much of my background material.

I would especially like to thank my mother, Patricia, now aged 92, for her help with names, chronology and places; my husband, Harry, for help with proof-checking and advice on printing, as well as for his patience when my housekeeping was overtaken by my literary tasks, so that meals arrived several hours late, and I crawled into bed at three in the morning!

My son, Jamie, read my first draft and gave me his warmest encouragement. My son, Simon, has designed and photographed the cover of this book with his own great talent for creative and sophisticated photography. My daughter, Arabella, has appropriately given me a new grandchild, Angus, born exactly one hundred years after her sailor grandfather. (Her first baby, and my seventh grandchild.)

And so I give them, all three, my loving thanks, as well as to their wives Sarah and Aurora, and to Arabella's husband, Jamie Maudslay.

On the professional side, my special thanks go to the enthusiastic team at Buccleuch Printers in Hawick who have "built" my book for me, and to Alanna Knight's daughter-in-law who typed the first draft while awaiting the birth of her own first baby, Chloe.

Finally, my deepest thanks of all must go to Admiral Sir Julian Oswald and Richard Hough for so generously giving my book "a fair wind".

# INTRODUCTION

———————

I BEGAN TO WRITE these recollections on the fiftieth anniversary of the outbreak of the Second World War. What better day to start setting down my childhood memories as the daughter of a naval officer?

"My War" was probably not much different to anyone else's war. And yet, as a sailor's daughter, and with a brother in the Navy as well, I felt as though I was closely involved in the defence of Britain, even though I was only eleven years old when the war began.

The Navy was in my bloodstream, for we had moved wherever my father was sent. Home ports like Portsmouth, Chatham, and Devonport; Liverpool when his ship had to be refitted in Cammell Laird's yard; and Rosyth during the final years of his naval career, when he reached the dizzy heights as an admiral and became C-in-C Scotland and Northern Ireland. At most of these ports there had been frightening air-raids. It almost seemed as though the Luftwaffe had a private vendetta with us. They very nearly got us, in the end, ironically, at our own home on the Clyde.

We had travelled extensively, to South Africa for two and a half years; and, then, three years later, leaving my brother at school in Britain (as was the harsh custom of the day and age, in the 1930's) to China, to join my father who had been sent there as Senior Naval Officer, West River, with a flotilla of gunboats under his command.

Like all sailors' families, my brother and I soon got used to our many moves from rented house to rented house, and we were quite unaware that our mother felt perpetually frustrated by the task of turning other people's houses and gardens into a comfortable home for us, which she did superbly well. Everything was new and exciting for me, which is why my childhood became so indelibly stamped in every detail on my mind, so that I can remember it all to this day. Much of the time we spent with grandparents and cousins while my father was at sea, and this was part of the life of a sailor's daughter, as well as the more exciting travels

Perhaps the most exciting time of all was when we were in China in 1937, living in Canton when the Japanese started to bomb that huge and bustling Chinese city in 1938.

Our sense of the presence of the British Empire in those days was a fact of life. No-one imagined for a moment that the Empire would ever be dismantled. But my father had inherited a liberal point of view from his Scottish ancestors, who had all been diehard Whigs. He was like his great-great uncle, the Hon. Mountstuart Elphinstone (younger brother of Lord Elphinstone), a Governor of Bombay and an enlightened administrator in India at the start of the nineteenth century, who ended his brilliant career with an invitation from the government of his day to be Viceroy of India, but turned the offer down, because he was determined to write a definitive "History of India". Elphinstone wanted to explain to future administrators how the complicated structure of the Indian continent was made up, and he also wanted to emphasise the point that British administrators were sent to India to *help* the Indians, and not to patronise them.

My father held the same views when posted overseas by their Lordships of the Admiralty. His duties as a captain of gunboats on the West River not only included his duty to protect international traders under the dictates of the 1840 Treaty of Nanking, by which western countries had given money and technical help to China, and in return were allowed to take revenue from resulting trade, with gunboats to supervise on the Yangtse and the West River, but also to help the Chinese in any way that he possibly could. I suspect that he was one of very few naval officers who felt that the second part of his "remit" was almost certainly the most important. His own feeling was that, as he was temporarily living in someone else's country, so his behaviour to his hosts, the Chinese, should be as punctilious as that of a guest staying in someone else's house.

My reason for writing my memories of a fascinating childhood as a sailor's daughter, is not so much an "ego trip", but a means of describing for posterity the very different world we lived in during the 1930's and 1940's, which has already become "history". General interest in personal memoirs must necessarily provide an interest in 'social history', and I hope that my vivid childhood memories may contribute a few more stitches to the constantly unfolding tapestry of life. I also think my grandchildren may find it rather amusing.

There will be many repetitions and inaccuracies, for which I apologise in advance. My father's own short verse which he quotes at the beginning of his privately printed naval memoirs applies no less to me:

"With assurance they state recollections
Of deeds of the days of their youth.
Which memory's known imperfections
Must rob of some semblance of truth."

Most of the memories in this book are exclusively my own, but I have dipped into two other works for encouragement and assistance, the first being Jan Morris's trilogy on the rise and decline of the British Empire, which provided me with important background material from her brilliant panorama of history, "glorious, savage, sad and painful", of which my own childhood only occupied the blink of an eyelid, the flash of butterflies' wings, the fall of a snowflake, or the glimmer of a ray of sunshine on a cobweb.

The second work has been my father's own memoirs of his naval career, *Random Naval Recollections,* from which I have extracted aspects of his career of which I was quite unaware at the time, and which must essentially set the scene for my own childhood, "before the mast", as a sailor's daughter. The photograph book, in which my mother wrote pithy remarks about my childhood, has also been quite invaluable.

For this reason, my book is written in memory of a unique and much-loved father, who taught us that life was *fun.* He also taught us that it is possible to enjoy every job you are given to do in life, however unpromising it may seem at first. I pass this useful tip on to my grandchildren, it might be helpful to them one of these days.

His sailor's upbringing and training had been strict, so we, too, were given rules to be obeyed. Occasionally, he had to reprimand us; but always in a quiet, sympathetic voice, which I found totally demoralising, because we knew we had let him down. My chief childhood memory is of laughter and foolish fun, alternating with intense pride when I saw my father standing on his own quarterdeck, telescope under his arm, legs braced against the heaving of the deck, and his sailor's eyes looking towards the far horizon across white-capped waves.

The back-cloth of my childhood was undoubtedly the white ensign, a ship's band, the whooping of destroyers, and smartly dressed sailors saluting my father with their chirping bosun's pipes as he came aboard. I was a sailor's daughter, and I was proud of it.

Easter Harden
*August 1993*

# CUNNINGHAME GRAHAM FAMILY

## GRANDFATHERS

Robert Cunninghame Graham of
Gartmore and Finlaystone
b. 1799, 8th Laird. *The family
descended directly from King
Robert The Bruce, through the
Graham earls of Menteith.*

*m. 1824*

## GRANDMOTHERS

Frances Laura Speirs of Elderslie
*grand-daughter of 1st Baron Dundas,
and great-grand-daughter
of Earl Fitzwilliam.*

William Cunninghame Graham
Bontine of Ardoch, Gartmore
and Finlaystone b. 1825 (9th Laird).

*m. 1851*

Hon. Anne Elizabeth Elphinstone
Fleeming, *daughter of Admiral The
Hon. Charles Elphinstone-Fleeming
(younger brother of 11th Lord
Elphinstone), and Dona Catalina
Alessandro of Cadiz.*

Commander Charles Cunninghame
Graham (second son of above)
b. 1854 *younger brother of R. B.
Cunninghame Graham, 10th Laird
of Gartmore, writer, politician,
traveller and horseman. Charles
served in the Royal Navy until 1887,
when he became Deputy Chief
Inspector of the R.N.L.I. (Lifeboats),
Groom-in-Waiting to King Edward VII,
and Equerry to King George V (1906–1917).*

*m. 1882*

Mildred Emily Barbara Bagot,
*daughter of Rev. Charles Walter
Bagot, Rector of Castle Rising, Norfolk.
Her nephew, Caryl Ernest, became 6th
Baron Bagot of Blithfield,
Staffordshire.*

## PARENTS

Angus Cunninghame Graham
b. 1893. *His sister was Olave
Clementina, married to Basil Brooke.*

*m. 1924*

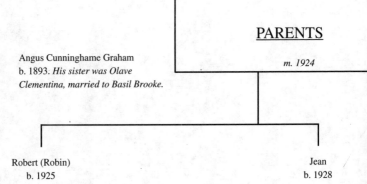

Robert (Robin)
b. 1925

Jean
b. 1928

First cousin: Basil (Bil) Brooke.

# HANBURY FAMILY

## GRANDFATHERS

## GRANDMOTHERS

Robert Hanbury of Poles,
Hertfordshire, b. 1798 *younger
brother of Osgood Hanbury of
Holfield Grange.*

*m. 1819*

Emily Hall his cousin *daughter of
William Hall.*

George Hanbury *third son of above*
of Blythewood, Bucks. b. 1829.

*m. 1857*

Mary Trotter *eldest daughter of
Capt. John Trotter of Dyrham Park,
Hertfordshire.*

Lionel Hanbury, b. 1864
of Hitcham House, Bucks.,
formerly Blythewood.
*Director of the Bank of England,
Lieutenant of the City of London.*

*m. 1891*

Margaret Colmore Allhusen
*daughter of Henry Christian Allhusen
of Stoke Court, Bucks. Her family
originated in Schleswig Holstein,
Denmark, in the early 19th century
when Carl Christian Friedrick
Allhusen, a merchant from Denmark,
started a chemical business in
Newcastle-upon-Tyne, and lived at
Elswick Hall.*

Mary Patricia Hanbury
b. 1901. *Her brothers and sisters were Reginald, Betty, Rachel,
and Christopher, married respectively to:
Esmé Fitzroy, Kit Riley, Herbert Fitzherbert and Lettice Charrington.*

First cousins: Nicholas and Bill Fitzherbert.
Andalusia and John Riley. Ben, Juliet and David Hanbury.
Reg and Bob Hanbury.

# CHAPTER I

———◆———

ON MY PASSPORT it says that I was born on 20th May 1928 at a place called Westbourne. More times than I can remember I have had to copy this piece of information out on to little forms handed to me by air-hostesses or customs officials, but it was only very recently that I bothered to look the place up on the map. Imagine my surprise and delight when I found that it was only a few miles from Portsmouth! If I was not to be born in Scotland, from which country my father's ancestors had sprung, then surely Portsmouth was exactly the right place for me to make my entrance into the world, as a sailor's daughter.

On returning from Malta in 1928, where my father had been first lieutenant of the *Royal Sovereign,* he was promoted to Commander and appointed to the Tactical School in Portsmouth. His job was to lecture to captains and admirals on naval tactics, and they usually attended the courses between appointments. My father used to say that these exalted naval officers behaved exactly like schoolboys, as soon as they found themselves in a classroom, writing each other private notes, surreptitiously reading books, and showing obvious inattention. He soon discovered that the one way to bring the class to life was to make a deliberate mistake, and, just like schoolboys, the captains and admirals were delighted to be able to catch out their teacher. During the course he received copies of "Orders

1

for Tactical Exercises at Sea", most of which came from Admiral Dudley Pound who was C-in-C of the Mediterranean Fleet. The orders were so voluminous and detailed that even the enemy was told what to do, and no-one was given any scope for initiative, which did not seem to be the right way of going about things, to my father.

Lying in my pram in the garden of our house at East Ashling (Westbourne turned out to be merely the place where my birth had been registered, a few miles away), I am told that I was aware only of the nightingales singing. This I have to take on trust from my mother, as I cannot positively say that I have ever heard a nightingale sing in Britain.

My parents and three-year-old brother, Robin, had only just returned from a two-year posting to Malta, where I was, presumably, conceived.

It was generally agreed that I was so ugly that the only person I resembled at all was our erstwhile Maltese cook. As my mother had haemorrhaged severely during my birth, she was far too weak and tired to find this the least bit amusing. On the other hand, and fortunately for me, Nanny (who had looked after Robin in Malta), thought I was quite beautiful. She was also delighted to be living in West Sussex, where she could keep in touch with her uncle in nearby Hampshire, to go for expeditions in the sidecar of his motorbike on her days off. Sometimes, I went home with Nanny, when I was older, to see her pet jackdaw, "Jackie", who talked almost as clearly as a parrot. Poor Jackie came to an untimely end when he fell into a bucket of water and was drowned, admiring his own reflection.

It was Nanny's uncle, several years later, who made me my doll's house. It had running water, which flowed from the taps in the bathroom when you poured a jug of cold water into the cistern in the roof. Next to the cistern there was a place for a torch battery, and when this was fixed up, lights shone through the windows of the doll's house from every room. It was truly magical, and I never quite forgave myself for my impulsive gesture during the Second World War, as a teenager,

2

when I bequeathed it to a Scottish orphanage. I only hope the orphans loved it as much as I did.

Nanny, being the only person who did not think I was an ugly baby, immediately started to cherish me with her very loving heart. Her voice was the first sound I can positively remember, and I can still hear her soft Hampshire accent to this day, like the coo-ing of a dove. She was small and round, with twinkly eyes, an ample bottom, and a bosom like two firm pillows.

By the time I was a few months old, I was taken in the car to watch my father playing cricket, wrapped up in innumerable shawls over my long white lawn baby-clothes, which Nanny had spent hours starching, ironing, and goffering, just like Mrs Tiggy Winkle, who she resembled so closely.

Nanny and I would be arranged on the back seat of the rather grand car we owned, which was a relic of my father's carefree bachelor days, and was known as "The Bean", or "The Haricot Royale", because it had come from my uncle, Basil Brooke, who was an equerry to the Duke of York.

Robin bounced up and down beside us, wearing an attractive linen suit like Christopher Robin. Lots of small boys were called Robin then, and it was not until he became a naval cadet that he decided to protest, and to use his real name, Robert, which was the name borne most frequently by our forebears, the Grahams of Gartmore, who descended directly from King Robert the Bruce of Scotland. The most distinguished member of our family, our great uncle, Robert Bontine Cunninghame Graham, the writer, politician, and horseman, was not to end his long and colourful life for another seven years.

The cricket matches took place at the house of my father's friend, Algie Bonham Carter, in Petersfield. The house was called Buriton, and it was there that Gibbon had written his interminable *Decline and Fall*. Algie Bonham Carter was the local squire, and as such, he provided a cricket ground, and used to invite visiting sides to play his local team. His own were particularly accurate at bowling, having practised the art by throwing stones at the squire's pheasants, with which they surreptitiously provided themselves throughout the winter. As a result, they could throw down the wicket from almost anywhere in the field.

The most exciting match of the season was the one played against a team from the Royal Yacht. Three of my father's greatest friends were amongst the players in 1928; Tom Troubridge, Tom Halsey, and "Monkey" Sellar. The players got so excited that Monkey Sellar was caught out by the umpire, at square leg, which confused the scoring somewhat. At these matches, my father always kept the wicket.

Watching cricket at the age of two or three months must have influenced me more than anyone could have imagined, for cricket was to become the only sport I ever really enjoyed. When I was fifteen, at my boarding school, I adored batting; this was chiefly because girls are normally quite unable to throw a ball, so our fiercest and fastest bowler merely gave me the opportunity to show off my ability to hit boundaries, the ball arriving nice and slowly, so that I could easily judge my stroke.

Unfortunately, I remember nothing about those early cricket matches at Petersfield, neither do I remember our move to a house near Sevenoaks where I celebrated my first birthday. The house had apparently been built by Lutyens for his own use – a fact that was of little interest to a child of barely a year old. But perhaps something of this great architect's style did brush off on me; for, fifty years later, when I saw Delhi for the first time, I was stunned by the simplicity of line which was the secret of his impact. I shall never forget the triumphal arch which stands at the heart of New Delhi, bearing the one hopeful word of unity "INDIA". Architecture undoubtedly has the power to inspire great political ideals, just as art and literature can do. India is still far from united, but Lutyen's arch is always there as a reminder.

At this point, my father attended the Naval Staff College at Greenwich, so he commuted from Sevenoaks to London every day. Towards the end of his life he used to tell us that the time he spent at the three Service Staff Colleges gave him an unparalleled education, chiefly from living and working with officers from the other two services, as well as from being with men who came to the colleges from overseas. But, on the other hand, he never felt himself to be quite "staff college material". He found that his ideas seldom coincided with those of his instructors, and what seemed quite clear to them was often totally obscure to him. He was convinced that they lived in a land of "make believe", inventing war-games, and quite unable to plan for the realities of war.

He told us of a disturbing example, when the three staff colleges – Navy, Army and Air Force – had all been set a theme, for their courses in 1929, on how to keep the Japanese out of Singapore in the event of a war with that country: the *"staff"* answer was; *a)* to strengthen the sea defences by adding more and larger coastal guns and defence craft, *b)* to increase the number of submarines and add extra minefields off the coast, *c)* to provide plenty of torpedo planes and bombers to take part in the defence of the coast from an invading force, and finally, *d)* to bring large numbers of troops to the possible landing points.

Not *one* of the staff college instructors ever considered that the Japanese might come in at the *"back door"*, as they were to do with such devastating results in the Second World War.

We left Sevenoaks in 1930, shortly after my second birthday, when my father moved on from the Naval Staff College to the Army Staff College at Camberley. We went to live in a house called College Farm – the second move in the first two years of my life. Camberley provided me with my first glimmer of a far-off memory. It concerns a donkey, and a vivid picture of Nanny bending over it to alter Robin's stirrups, while I sat watching from my pram. I am certain that the donkey winked at me before turning his head to take a nip at the temptingly large backside, clad in a grey skirt, within inches of its front teeth.

"Oh my goodness!" said Nanny, who was not prone to bad language, and she turned and slapped the donkey on the nose, at the same time rubbing her bottom.

"Oh my goodness! What a naughty donkey you are, Peter!"

Once Nanny took me to a meet of the Garth Hunt at Camberley, where we saw my father and mother looking exquisite on their hunters – my father wearing a black top hat, and my mother riding in a smart bowler. Robin had been allowed to attend the meet on Peter. He must have been an unusual sight on his donkey in woolly leggings and white galoshes, amongst all the grand huntin' folk. Obviously, the local press thought so too, and his picture was published in the local paper, helping himself to plum cake from a silver salver before the hounds moved off.

At the age of four, Robin was everyone's idea of the perfect small boy, with his curly hair and deceptively angelic good looks. At that stage, I was, according to the family photograph book, a friendly, plump, brown-haired, greeny-eyed "nondescript" sort of baby, with a large vocabulary for my age, and a strong sense of curiosity in the world about me. I was particularly fond of flowers, and one of the first photographs shows me, on my second birthday, standing proudly beside a basket of carnations given to me by our cook and housemaid. It was a strange birthday present for a two-year-old, but the expression on my face shows all too clearly how delighted I was.

My mother, who had always loved riding, was able to join a course at the Staff College for officers' wives, taken by an instructor from the Army School of Equitation at Weedon. This was how she learnt to jump huge fences, leading her on to enter an international horse-show, in Cape Town, two years later, which she very nearly won.

The Staff College Drag Hunt used to gallop past the back of our garden, at Camberley. There was a particularly notorious jump at that point, and I would stand on tip-toe at the garden fence, gleefully chanting "Horsey hop up! – Horsey hop down! – Man fall off!"

I have already mentioned the fact that I was a talkative child, and, on being taken by my mother, in my best coat and velvet bonnet, to watch the Passing Out Parade at Sandhurst, apparently my raucous and excited voice echoed across the parade-ground, as I caught a glimpse of a portly general wearing a kilt, "Mummy, dere's a Scotch boy!" I shouted, to her deep embarrassment.

Being in a place where a great many young officers passed by every day as they went about their classes, I was definitely obsessed with "the boys" – as Nanny called them. My mother used to stick our snapshots into photograph albums, and one day I was showing one of her friends the latest album after tea, when my mother distinctly heard me say, rather briskly, "No boys. Turn over".

But my own memories do not really begin to formulate clearly until just before my third birthday. In May 1931, we sailed in the *Dunbar Castle* to South Africa. My father had been appointed Commander of a light cruiser, H.M.S. *Cardiff*. He was overjoyed to be at sea once more, after being shore-based for nearly three years, and in April 1931 the *Cardiff* left Chatham for South Africa.

My mother, Robin, Nanny and I sailed to Cape Town a few weeks later, in our ship of the Union Castle Line. The only thing I remember about the whole voyage was a large and mysterious parcel which lurked in our four-berth cabin. Naval officers' wives did not travel first class in those days. On 20th May 1931, my third birthday, I was allowed to unwrap the parcel; it was a beautiful red and blue "bike", with pedals on the front wheel and large rubber tyres. I was ecstatic with joy. This was even better than carnations.

# CHAPTER II

L IVING IN A FOREIGN country, as a small child, allowed me to identify totally and unconditionally with my new environment. A child is continuously learning and copying all the strange quirks of the normal adult world, many of which seem totally illogical and incomprehensible, so it was no more difficult for me to learn about a different way of life, on a new continent and in a new hemisphere. As a result, because I could not remember a time when I had not known and loved black people, I had no hang-ups about them.

Our dark brown Cape-coloured maid was really called Gertrude. My own fond nickname for her was "Rosebud". She was someone with whom I had immediately forged a bond. I could not understand why the grown-ups found it so funny that I should call her Rosebud. I thought she was very kind, and very pretty. Our Zulu cook, Samson, seemed enormous to me and I was rather in awe of him – not because he was black, but because he had a great presence. Also, he did not like having little girls in his kitchen, so I used to be constantly shooed out. I was convinced that he was the same Samson as the one in the Bible, who was strong enough to pull down the pillars of the temple.

It seems strange to think that my mother laboriously taught Samson to make Shepherd's Pie, Toad-in-the-Hole, and steamed Canary Pudding. It is even stranger to think that we could have eaten things like that in such a hot climate, especially when the Cape provided so much delicious fish, and so many different kinds of exotic fruit.

From babyhood, I was excessively fond of my food and it played a great part in my life. Best of all, I liked mealies (corn on the cob), and the next greatest treat was to have paw-paw (or papaya) for breakfast.

More than fifty years later, I was to stay with my Colombian daughter-in-law, Aurora, in Caracas, and watched her giving their baby son paw-paw every day. "It contains all the right vitamins", she explained, "and it's easy to digest. In South America, we always give paw-paw to cure tummy upsets!" Perhaps it was our English nanny who had insisted on the English meals in South Africa, determined to avoid giving us strange local produce, of which she was uncertain and suspicious. Paw-paw would definitely have come into that category.

When we first arrived at our house outside Simonstown it was my beautiful scarlet and blue "bike" that was literally to be my downfall. We were the proud possessors of a long, wide, "stoep", or verandah, which overlooked a beautiful sandy bay. At one end of the stoep there was a flight of steps down which I confidently sped on my bike. Inevitably I ended up with a nasty bump on my head, and Nanny had to rub it with her magic cure-all ointment, which went by the name of "Pomade Divine". Once I had recovered I started to run about singing "Pom-mard-da-vine", over and over again. It was a beautiful word, I thought.

South Africa was to be home for me for the next two years. I wasn't a bit afraid of the sleepy snake that curled up in the sun under the stoep, and I have to this day always been far more frightened of mice and large moths. I also liked the other sort of snake which lived in a tree in our garden and was called a "Boomslang". Here was an Afrikaans word that was also delightful to chant, even better than "Pomade Divine". I soon started to pick up some more Afrikaans words, chiefly from a small boy called Tertius, who attended my brother's school. In our garden there were weaver birds, which made strange nests for themselves like string bags, hanging from the trees. There were also always large numbers of pretty sugar birds in our garden.

Nanny used to take us for long walks after lunch each day, just as she did in England. Sometimes I was allowed to go in the push-chair, if it was raining, with the hood up. I called it my "lid". I can remember being pushed down a long avenue of trees, and seeing weaver birds' nests hanging down from every tree, in festoons.

But best of all was the beach. It was the most perfect beach for small children that I have ever known. Sheltered from the strong Atlantic gales with soft white sand, its smooth boulders gave it the name "Boulders Beach". The sea was always a brilliant blue-green with a soft, frothing white edge to it, where the baby breakers fizzled out in the sand. On the other side of Cape Point was the Indian Ocean, which was much warmer for bathing.

To feel the sand between my toes was a sensation I shall never forget, made all the more perfect by the contrast of the short prickly path we had to negotiate (usually in bare feet) to get from our garden to the beach. Most people from Cape Town went to the wide beach at Muizenberg to surf, so, at Simonstown we usually had the Boulders Beach to ourselves.

"Put your shoes on, you tinkers!", Nanny would exhort Robin and me from the "stoep", as we dashed down to the sandy bay. But it was too much bother, and I could never get that horrid little shiny shoe-button to go through the tight eyehole at the end of the strap.

My chief delight on the beach was to look for shells. They came in the most delicate colours: pale yellows, pinks and mauves, fan-shaped, and about the size of a small finger-nail. My cotton frocks, made by Nanny, had large pockets which I used to fill with shells. I called them my "saving shells", because I saved them in a special cardboard box.

It was at this time that my Hanbury grandfather sent me a book – it was called "The Pirate Twins", and I was delighted to

11

find that it was about a little girl who discovered a tiny pair of pirate twins in a shell on the beach. I soon knew the words of the whole book by heart and could "read" it to my mother at bedtime. Another book I loved was called *Josephine and her Dolls*. I am convinced that it was due to those two books that I learnt to read very soon after my fourth birthday. Since then, I have never ceased to devour as many books as I can lay my hands on. Reading has always been my chief delight throughout my life; always a comfort and an "escape" at moments of stress, as I was quickly to tell my own children in due course.

Before we arrived in Simonstown, I was probably quite unaware that my father was a sailor. The shore jobs he had been given during the first three years of my life were not very obviously "nautical", to a small child. Now my father was the commander of a light cruiser of around 5,000 tons; and, as such, he had an extremely arduous and responsible job as the executive officer of his ship.

My first memory of the *Cardiff* was dancing to the ship's band. I need hardly mention that the ship's march was the Welsh tune, "Men of Harlech". Robin and I sang our own version, which had nothing to do with the bawdy words that the sailors themselves substituted. We used to march round the garden singing "Men of Harlech, gorging garlic . . ." giggling helplessly at our own amazing wit.

A large number of sixteen-year-old "boys" were amongst the crew of the *Cardiff*, from the training ship *Arethusa*. My mother decided they were probably feeling very home-sick, so they all came to tea at "The Boulders". They enjoyed the very English atmosphere of our house, and I suspect that the reason they were so nice to Robin and me was because they were missing their own young brothers and sisters rather badly.

It was almost too good to be true, to be sitting on the knee of one of these large handsome boys, who looked so devastating in their bell-bottoms, and I was given far too much attention for my own good. The tea-party always ended with a hilarious game of rounders on the beach, when the boys forgot they were in the Navy, and remembered, instead, the happy days spent with their families at the seaside in England.

On Sundays, we used to go to church on board H.M.S. *Cardiff*. In true naval tradition, the Captain took the service and the ship's band played the hymns. It could not have been a more inspiring way to introduce a child to church-going. I particularly remember the Sunday when a school of "yellow tail" fish came close in to the cruiser during the Morning Service, and the local fishermen started hauling them in every fifteen seconds, off the "Bull's Nose" as the mole at Simonstown was called. The whole congregation was transfixed by the scene, until the Naval padre said, rather crossly, in the middle of his sermon, "Haven't you ever seen a fish caught before?" Afterwards at lunch, my father declared that the padre had missed the perfect opportunity to tell the parable of the draught of fishes.

By the time I was four-years-old, I was well-accustomed to the thrilling sound of the Bosun's pipe, saluting my father, the ship's Commander, as he came on board. I soon got used to the official reception at the top of the companion way, and I probably thought it was entirely for my own benefit, as I usually followed closely behind him when we went on board.

I had already attended several children's parties on board the *Cardiff*, and as everyone will know who understands the British sailor's deep love of children, these were always particularly exciting and happy occasions. Everything possible was done by the ship's company to amuse their small guests. They donned pirates' scarves and cutlasses for the event, with black patches over one eye, and dirks tucked into colourful sashes. The Skull and Crossbones flew from the main mast, and the ship was "dressed overall", which meant that she was decorated from stem to stern with coloured flags.

Sometimes we were ushered into a "pirate's cave" to receive "gold doubloons" made of chocolate; or, we would be invited to dip our hands into a bucket of water through which a very small electric current flowed, to see if we were brave enough to pick out the small coins at the bottom of the bucket, with its strangely "fizzy" sensation. Another entertainment the sailors arranged for us was a slide made out of a canvas wind-tunnel, or a realistic rocking horse, knocked up for the occasion by a ship's "chippy". There was always a huge spread of sandwiches, jellies, ice-cream and chocolate biscuits, and usually a small present and a balloon for each child, as they went ashore at the end of the party. I remember being given a beautiful little sewing box, which started me off on the delight of making dolls' clothes, although my first attempts looked rather odd, with huge, irregular stitches, and turning out more like small sacks, with holes for the arms and legs.

For my fourth birthday, after we had been in South Africa for nearly a year, I had my own birthday party on board the *Cardiff*. The two things that stand out in my memory about that day are, first of all, the exquisite mauve birthday cake (the colour specially commanded by me) made by the ship's chef; and, secondly, the enormous row I had with my mother while dressing for the party, when I insisted on wearing bright green socks with my pale pink organdie party frock.

We had a family rule that no-one was allowed to be thwarted on their birthday, but my mother contrived a tactful compromise – I was to be photographed before we left home, wearing my green socks, after which I would change into white ones. I think the day must have been cold (May being the first of the winter months in South Africa), for I particularly remember wearing a chilprufe vest under my organdie frock, and standing still for what seemed like hours, while Nanny pinned the sleeves of my vest out of sight, under some frills of organdie, with small gold safety pins.

The *Cardiff* had, by this time, become my second home, and my brother and I were atrociously spoilt by the ship's company. When she went off for periodic exercises, to be away for several weeks at a time, we all felt very lonely and lost without her. The excitement on her return to Simonstown was intense; we always stood on the quay to greet her return, as she sailed in with her ship's band playing. Then there would be mysterious parcels to be unpacked from my father's luggage, to reveal carved African animals, bows and arrows, a tom-tom, and once even a real, full-sized native canoe, which we launched into the waves on the beach below our house. Another treasure was the pelt of a wild cat, my father had shot up the west coast of Africa at Lobito.

These cruises took the ship, often with an admiral on board, up the east coast of Africa to Port Elizabeth, East London and Durban, and on to Laurenco Marques and Madagascar. Up the west coast, they sailed past the Bight of Benin, which used to be so disease-ridden that the old catch says of it "the Bight of Benin, the Bight of Benin, from which few come out though many go in". From there, the *Cardiff* once steamed 70 miles up the Congo, and finally on to Accra and to Sierra Leone. Kenya had been annexed by the Royal Navy's East Indies station so that they could have a cooler mountainous place to go to on leave in extreme heat. My father admitted that he was disappointed that this part of Africa was not available to the *Cardiff*. In South Africa the climate was never too hot, and, in fact, it often grew quite chilly when the south-easterlies blew straight from the Antarctic.

My mother and father rode horses a great deal in the Cape, and my mother bravely took part in the Cape Province Horse Show at Rosebank, getting into the finals with a jump-off between herself and a South African girl called Vivian Van der Byl. My mother lost to Miss Van der Byl by half a fault, a result which allowed everyone to applaud a victory by their local girl, but also covered my mother with honour and glory. We all felt very proud of her. The jumps had looked colossal, but her horse, Trotsky, although difficult to ride, simply loved jumping.

My parents had made great friends with an Afrikaans family called Struben, and I started to learn to ride on a fat white pony of theirs, although, even at the age of five I knew that I was unlikely to follow in my mother's footsteps as a natural horsewoman. I was not sure that I even *liked* horses very much, which was strange, because I loved all other animals, especially dogs.

Another local family who were very kind to us were the Packers. Joy Packer was a well-known South African writer, married to an English naval officer. Their son, Piet, was the same age as me, and I can vividly remember the first time I went to tea with him. He had a German nanny (from Dresden) and we were given beautiful blue-handled skipping ropes, as small presents wrapped in coloured tissue paper and waiting for us on the tea table. I believe Piet is now a famous eye surgeon. Joy Packer's novels about the Navy, and later about South Africa, have always appealed to me greatly.

On one occasion my father and mother were at a lunch party given by the British C-in-C, Admiral Tweedie, in honour of the famous South African leader General Smuts, and his wife. In the middle of lunch, Mrs Smuts suddenly pointed at her husband and laughingly exclaimed, "Just look at your coat, Jan!". They all looked, and there, sewn on, was a large label with "Tweed coat 30/6d" on it!

It was at that lunch, that the General told my father how he had once, as a young man, repelled the British Navy single-handed, during the Boer War. He had been sitting on a cliff, above a little bay, when he saw a small British warship coming in, apparently intent on anchoring in the bay. When the ship got close, he fired two shots at her with his rifle, whereupon her captain turned and made off. General Smuts said he had felt very brave and very pleased with himself.

My brother was now at a small convent school in Simonstown, run by nuns, being the best educational establishment for both British and Afrikaans children in the area. At his school's end-of-term concert I was allowed to join in, by sitting on the front of his bike with him as we sang together:

"Daisy, Daisy, give me your answer do!
I'm half crazy, all for the love of you!
It won't be a stylish marriage,
For I can't afford the carriage,
But you'll look sweet, upon the seat,
Of a bicycle made for two!"

I was quite unaffected by stage fright, and had to be restrained from taking too many curtain calls, being carried away by the enthusiastic applause of the captive audience of parents.

Another song I learnt to sing was the Afrikaans song "Sari Marais", with its catchy tune; and I also knew a good number of popular songs by the time I was four, because Nanny had a portable wireless, which was still quite a new-fangled invention in those days.

One of the songs which I remember best of all, brought me as near as I ever got to knowing about the Depression, which had been at its height both in Britain and the United States the year after I was born, in 1929. The chorus of the popular song (which was the equivalent of "Top of the Pops", in its day) went:

> "No more money in the bank,
> No more babies left to spank,
> What to do about it?
> Let's put out the lights and go to bed."

An important world event took place while we were in South Africa. Britain came off the Gold Standard. The grown-ups looked worried, and were constantly talking about it, although I hadn't the faintest idea what it meant. I was convinced it must have something to do with the flag called the Royal Standard which Nanny told me King George V flew, on a huge flag pole, over Buckingham Palace. She said it was gold, and it only flew when he was at home. Everyone seemed so upset about its disappearance that I wondered if perhaps the King had gone away for good. My feelings of anxiety and foreboding were a strange premonition of the approaching end of the British Empire. Grown-ups seldom realise that children are keenly aware of important world events, even though they may not completely understand the full implications of them. (Rather the same as dogs sensing earthquakes, I suppose.) This disaster affected us personally, for every gold sovereign my father was paid by their Lordships at the Admiralty, he only received 14 shillings and 6 pence.

During the time we spent in South Africa, we led a very simple life. I was perfectly content to play with my dolls endlessly on the beach, or hunt for shells, and I never minded being alone when Robin was at school, for I was a solitary child with a very vivid imagination, and I always had plenty going on in my head to keep me amused. My dolls were all very real to me, and I carried on long conversations with them, as I dressed them in the clothes Nanny made for them, for my dolls' tea-parties.

I believed implicitly in fairies, as all Celtic people do, and found them both in the exotic flowers in our garden, and even more so in the sea-shells on the beach, which were exactly the colours of fairies' wings.

We had an orange cat called Musty (I think he was originally called Mustard), and two pet chameleons who lived on the electric light shade over the dining-room table, and caught flies, which were their staple diet. They were strange primitive little creatures, and although I was fascinated by their ability to change colour at will, taking on their camouflage from their background, I was really rather frightened of them, especially when my mother let me hold them. I hated their quick movements and the tickly feeling as they rushed up my arm. I would far rather have had a dog, but that was impossible in Africa because of rabies. My mother promised me one as soon as we got back to England.

I did not want to go back to England, *ever*, but I did want a dog very badly. It was the first time I can remember thinking that I had to make this important decision myself. I was totally unaware that I should be very unlikely to be consulted. At the time, I was quite convinced that it was my decision, alone.

I can well remember, at the age of four, that it seldom occurred to me to ask grown-ups for help or advice. If I had to do up my own shoe-laces, I struggled on until they were done, and refused to let Nanny re-tie my somewhat unorthodox knots, which were then impossible to undo again. I must have been a maddening child. But I learnt my lesson one day when I tried to pick the prickly-pears in our garden, which I had been told not to touch, and had to have the prickles scrubbed out of my hands by Nanny with a hard nail-brush.

Clothes were almost as important to me as food, and Nanny sewed beautifully, not only dolls' clothes, but mine as well, so I had plenty of pretty dresses to wear. She also made my sun bonnets, which I had to wear if I was playing on the beach. They were made of checked gingham and were called "poke bonnets", because they poked forward, shading my face as well as my head and neck.

The first time Nanny made one of these bonnets for me, I was only three, and we were going to tea in Simonstown with some friends who had a little boy the same age as me, called Reggie. Reggie was small and plump with a beaming smile and we loved each other very dearly. When Nanny tied my new bonnet under my chin, I felt smothered in checked gingham, and broke into a wail.

"What is it, darlin'?" asked Nanny mystified.

Between heart-rending sobs, I snuffled, "But . . . Nan . . . poor . . . Reggie . . . won't . . . be . . . able . . . to . . . kiss . . . me . . . in . . . dis . . . hat."

I couldn't understand why Nanny put her hands on her hips and laughed till she was quite pink in the face.

The colder weather came with the winter gales in June and July. I was dressed by Nanny in my winter clothes in the current English fashion: chilprufe vest and chilprufe bodice with buttons to which a skirt or kilt was attached, and a jersey over the top. My mother knitted beautifully and my proudest possession was a striped jersey she had made for me out of oddments of coloured wool. The bodice, which is a thing of the past, was, in fact, a very clever device for getting over the problems of a child's waistline – small boys' trousers were kept up by it; and it was a godsend for securing a kilt for both boys and girls. We were proud to be Scottish, even though we had not as yet gone to live in Scotland, due to my father's naval appointments being mainly in the south of England, so we loved to wear our kilts. My brother and I wore the Graham of Menteith tartan, which was our own family tartan.

My father had told me that our family was descended from the Kings of Scotland, and that there was still an old Graham castle in Perthshire that belonged to us. It was in ruins on a tiny island called Inch Talla, right in the middle of the Lake of Menteith. He explained that lakes in Scotland were usually called "lochs". Mary Queen of Scots, aged five, had arrived there, with her four little Mary's ("There was Mary Seaton, Mary Beaton, Mary Carmichael and me" as the song goes), and they had come there to be kept safe in the old island priory of Inchmahome until they sailed for France. The five children travelled in a litter, in a close cavalcade of horses, and as they approached their destination from the direction of Stirling Castle, the little queen is said to have exclaimed in delight, "Voila le lac!"

All of this appealed greatly to my romantic nature, and I longed to go to Scotland. Perhaps, after all, I would settle for a dog, and for Scotland, even if it did mean leaving my beloved South Africa.

Not all of our time was spent at the Boulders. My parents were quite adventurous and they wanted us to learn as young as possible how to cope with "roughing it". Poor Nanny was also involved in these expeditions, which cannot have been exactly her idea of fun. But she put up with the camping trips gamely, and pretended most convincingly that she was enjoying them as much as we did. When my father got a few days' leave from his ship, we set off, piled up with the camping gear, in our large oblong Dodge, and made for the mountains behind Cape Town. I am totally vague as to where we went, but I remember that it seemed quite a long drive, often bumping along unsurfaced roads with gates. The gates were usually opened for us by small piccaninnies who were rewarded with acid drops, which my father liked to call "acidulated tablets". He loved long, silly words, and thought them all the funnier when they sounded rather pompous.

We sang songs as we bumped along, usually "rounds': "My dame hath a lame tame crane", and "London's burning", and "A boat, a boat, unto the ferry, then we'll go over and be merry, and laugh and quaff and drink brown sherry". My mother was extremely musical and had once played a Mozart piano concerto, with a full orchestra, in London, when she was only fifteen. She also had a beautiful singing voice. I am sure my own love and understanding of music began to blossom on those journeys, as we learnt to sing and hold a part while the car bowled along the dusty red roads. On that trip I believe we went to a place called Ceres.

I remember much more vividly arriving at Jonker's Hoek, where we pitched the tents beside a beautifully clear stream that came down from the mountains. The stream was to be both our bathing pool (the sort I liked because it was not too deep) and also our "larder" for cooling our drinks. Nanny had brought a large jar of soup which she decided was vital for my lunch, and this, too, was wedged in the pool to keep fresh until the next day.

During the night we had a tropical storm, the rain poured down like bath-water and the river rose so that all our bottles, including my jar of soup, were washed away. My special sleeping place on these expeditions was the capacious back-seat of the car, while my mother and father shared one of the two small tents, and Nanny and Robin the other. Waking up in pitch darkness to hear the rain hitting the roof of the car like a machine gun, my mother heard my small voice above the noise, calling out indignantly,

"I can't see where I *are*!"

Strangely enough, I don't think I was particularly alarmed, although I was normally rather frightened of the dark. But I loved camping and was prepared to put up with all sorts of new and uncomfortable experiences without complaint, as long as Nanny and I were allowed to go too. I thought it very unfair if my parents went alone with Robin, which happened from time to time.

On one of these trips it was Nanny who stayed at home (perhaps to give her a much deserved rest), and instead of camping we slept in rondavels. Robin and I shared one, and were terrified when we spied an enormous spider climbing up the wall. We were convinced it was a tarantula.

We learnt a lot on those trips, and I can remember my father showing us how to set a compass; and pointing out the dangers of leaving empty bottles out in the open, because the hot sun shining through the glass could easily start a bush fire.

There was always a danger of poisonous snakes and insects wherever we camped, so we invariably carried an antidote with us, and my mother wore a whistle round her neck (even when we just went for ordinary picnics), just in case we had to summon help in an emergency. We were taught not to wander off alone since my mother and father had recently been to Bechuana to stay with the Earl and Countess of Moray, who had a house there. Their five-year-old son, Douglas, who was the same age as me, had got lost while taking their two ridgeback dogs for a walk, and was nearly eaten by a leopard. He was only discovered after a huge search. I was told that he later explained "I told the dogs to show me the way home but they just stayed beside me and wouldn't move!" Perhaps it was the close and loyal presence of the dogs that had really saved his life.

We were exposed to a great deal of sheer beauty on our camping trips, especially the wild flowers which grew in great profusion, large clusters of arum lilies, and small red gladioli, freesias and agapanthus – all growing wild. The protea was the "national flower", but they gave me the creeps, especially when I discovered that they were often home to a whole dynasty of ants.

There were orange and lemon groves and vineyards and distant blue hills, and always rondavels, which were the homes of the cheerful black Africans in their brightly coloured clothes, who never ceased to be friendly and welcoming to us.

Political problems for South Africa were far into the future at that time, although I feel sure there was plenty of injustice even then. I can distinctly remember the shanty towns that surrounded Cape Town where the black families must have been living in appalling poverty and deprivation. The greatest quality of the black African is his or her indomitable cheerfulness and high spirits, even under adversity, and this was one of the reasons South Africa, in those days, was such a happy place in which to live.

My father's ship was due to sail back to England in 1933 so we only had a few more months to spend in this idyllic country. Robin and I continued to play happily on the beach and in our garden. Robin had been given a Red Indian tent for his seventh birthday and we both dressed up with feathers in our hair and pitched our camp under the red flowering gum trees. In my father's privately published memoirs, written shortly before he died, he tells that "Robin and Jean could soon swim like fishes, once we got to South Africa". I fear he was deluding himself in my case: he had obviously forgotten the incident, shortly before we returned to England, when my mother had to dive in to rescue me from drowning because I had absent-mindedly walked out of my depth beneath the waves as I paddled my hands in the clear warm sea looking for shells. This episode made me even more frightened of learning to swim, and the phrase "out of my depth" became synonymous in my mind with being terrified out of my wits.

There was a battery of heavy guns behind our house, and once or twice a year they were tested. We were always warned beforehand and told to leave our windows open so that the glass would not shatter in the blast. My mother sensibly used to take us off for the day to have a picnic, knowing that the loud explosions could be extremely alarming. But one day she got the timing wrong, and, just as we had got home and were putting the car away in the garage, there was the loudest explosion I have ever heard to this day. Everything rattled and shook. On relating the story to Nanny, who had been on one of her rare days out, to Cape Town to window-shop at Stuttafords, I informed her that I had been "frightened out of my depth". The phrase was promptly co-opted into our family vocabulary to describe a state of intense terror.

Another cause for alarm during our time in South Africa were the frequent and spectacular thunderstorms. Nanny used to try to divert my attention by popping one of her supply of clear green peppermints into my mouth. She would get me out of bed and wrap me in a blanket, taking me to the windows to watch the sheet lightning (which I remember was bright pink) playing on a huge rock in the Bay. This frightened me more than ever, and I don't think she ever realised that I was far more frightened of the lightning than of the thunder itself. I knew about the thunder, because my father had told me quite plainly that thunder was only a silly old giant called Gumbleboo, falling downstairs, and I believed him implicitly. The lightning was totally incomprehensible and, as a result, much more terrifying. Intense fear is usually caused by something one doesn't understand – flying is a good example – and as soon as you know the underlying principles, it is always far less alarming.

When the time came for the *Cardiff* to return home, to my intense envy I found that seven-year-old Robin was to be allowed to travel home with my father in the *Cardiff* (I cannot see the Navy allowing such a thing to happen today!). My mother, Nanny and I were to follow soon afterwards in the Blue Funnel Line ship *Ulysses*. The final packing up, and the sad farewells to my dear brown "Rosebud" and to our Zulu cook were heartbreaking. They had become close friends. Several families came to see us off, and my chief memory is of the coloured streamers joining ship to shore in a maze of twisted ribbons as the band played, and we sailed away forever from South Africa.

On the voyage home, I was allowed to do the rounds with the steward who blew a bugle to summon the passengers to meals, accompanying him on my own toy trumpet. I also remember plunging into a canvas swimming pool with my mother who was still vainly trying to teach me to swim. I used to cling firmly to my rubber ring, shrieking, and in the end my mother decided that I must be the first child ever to have spent two years beside the most perfect beach in South Africa, and still unable to swim. Fortunately for me, it soon started to get colder, and the canvas swimming pool was finally taken down by the crew, to my great relief, and stowed away for use on the next voyage.

There was one memorable day on the homeward journey when I received a signal sent from my brother on board H.M.S. *Cardiff.* I don't suppose many seven-year-old boys can have had the chance to dispatch a signal from a naval ship to their five-year-old sister following behind on a liner – I felt immensely important.

On the way home, I asked Nanny what England was like – I had no memory of it whatsoever.

"Oh, it's a lovely *green* country, darlin'!" exclaimed Nanny, rapturously. When we arrived at the docks at Tilbury, in the Thames, downstream from London, I could see no sign of anything green. It was the only moment when my faith in my beloved Nanny was temporarily shaken.

The *Cardiff* had already arrived in Chatham, where my father had to take his ship into the dockyard for the first time, which is an unnerving experience for the Commander of a ship. If by any awful chance there happens to be a collision, then there is bound to be a Court Martial. Warships are expensive toys. Fortunately, my father managed to get into the dockyard without bumping anything, and Robin and I were soon reunited once more in the countryside near Windsor, the home of our Hanbury grandparents. It was here, at Hitcham House, that I began to realise that Nanny was right, England was indeed "a green and pleasant land" in the summer of 1933.

Robin had become impossibly self-important since his journey home in a warship. He had inevitably been the ship's "mascot" and this went somewhat to his head. He had also learnt to gamble with the sailors, playing "housey-housey" (bingo). My father was horrified when Robin dumped his winnings (around £6.00) on his bunk, at the end of the voyage. He had fondly imagined that the sailors had been playing card games like "Happy Families" with Robin. He had not realised that one of the reasons that children always love sailors is

25

because they are allowed to behave *like* sailors, with no "do's and don'ts", and no attempt at "speaking proper". Robin had learnt more than anyone guessed on his momentous voyage home. It had been the best adventure of his young life.

# CHAPTER III

———◆━◆◆━◆———

WHILE MY FATHER was waiting for his next appointment on our return to England, and while we were still homeless, we went to stay with our grandparents near Windsor. To be plunged into "country house living" after our comparatively simple life in South Africa was quite a shock to the system. But I took to it like a duck to water, and Nanny soon decided that it suited her pretty well, too.

Hitcham House was my mother's home. It was a huge, ugly, red brick Victorian monstrosity which I decided, at the age of five, was the most beautiful house in the world. It was always full of uncles and aunts and cousins – which added to the fun. Hitcham House had been built by my Hanbury great-grandfather, whose family had made their money as hop-merchants. My grandfather was one of eleven children, which was in the Quaker tradition. All the Buxtons, Gurneys and Hanburys had huge families and they all married each other, so my mother had literally hundreds of cousins, a fact she found so daunting that she soon gave up trying to keep in touch with them all. As a result, we knew very few of them, and I still meet second cousins from time to time, of whose existence I have been totally unaware.

The connection usually comes to light when we find a picture of Elizabeth Fry hanging in our bedroom, if we are staying with friends who turn out to be relations. Elizabeth Fry (née Gurney) was the outstanding prison reformer who is the family "heroine", giving us all a very special feeling of belonging to a great family, in numbers as well as in deeds! The greatest surprise of all was when I was later to discover that my second husband's grandmother had been a Buxton. No wonder we had so much in common!

While normally considering myself to be Scottish, I have to admit that I have many more English cousins than Scottish ones. Robin and I used to think we were vastly superior, having a Scottish name, Cunninghame Graham, and would say rather rudely and patronisingly to my mother, as though we were totally unconnected to her, "But you're *English*!"

We were pretty two-faced about it, in fact, because we both loved Hitcham; and our Hanbury first-cousins were like additional brothers and sisters, of whom we became immensely fond.

Very recently I celebrated an auspicious birthday with a large family party, in a house which belongs to a cousin just across the road from Hitcham – the old house now being converted into flats for prosperous London commuters. Just before the party began, I decided to wander round Hitcham by myself to revive childhood memories. Who should I meet on my solitary pilgrimage, doing exactly the same thing, but my brother Robin.

It is difficult to know why we all loved Hitcham so much. It must have been partly due to the home-making talent of our grandmother. My grandmother was born an Allhusen, and her grandfather had settled in Newcastle from Schleswig Holstein in the mid-nineteenth century to start a chemical works, a forerunner of I.C.I. He had arrived in Britain before the annexation of Schleswig Holstein to Germany, so he was born a Dane. This was why Grannie had the pale hair of a Viking, which went silvery white at a very young age, just as mine has done. What a strange collection of genes I must have, from the Pictish origins of the Grahams, the Hertfordshire and Worcestershire heritage of the Hanburys, to the Spanish of my paternal great-grandmother, and the Danish of my maternal grandmother – never was there more of a mix of northern and southern blood.

As a girl, Grannie was very beautiful, and in old age she had a delicate grace which was fascinating to a small child. She was born with perfect taste, and was a brilliant manager, Hitcham, with all its many servants, running like clockwork, and everything always just right, with huge bowls of scented flowers and delicious food. In the drawing-room there were chairs of all sizes and degrees of comfort, including a large sofa known as "Lethe"; and, for five-year-olds, a chair with a seat in petit-point worked by Grannie showing "The Little Red Fox" from a children's book we all adored. The nursery wing was just as it should be, with all the old toys and a beautiful rocking horse on which I rode incessantly, finding it a great deal safer than a real pony. There was also a large night nursery which I shared with Nanny.

The main bedrooms were luxurious, with thick carpets and huge comfortable beds. Each bedroom had its own fireplace, and some unfortunate young "tweenie" (the "between floors maid') had to refill the coal scuttle every day, as well as carry up cans of hot water first thing in the morning, empty the slops, and replenish the large cold water jugs and the drinking-water carafes.

But Grannie was extremely fond of her servants, as they were proud to be called in those days. "She was always so kind to 'us unders'", an elderly retired kitchen-maid from the old days at Hitcham told me, not long ago. The servants' hall, the kitchens and the butler's pantry were the happiest places for children to be in that huge house, and it was always accepted that the children of the family were warmly welcomed "downstairs", as well as "upstairs", so we had the best of both worlds. The male staff consisted of the butler, called Massey, and his young assistant, the footman, a lively and handsome young man, Bertram, whom we called "Beetroot", because of his bright red cheeks – I suspect he had just as much fun romping with the pretty young housemaids as he did, more innocently, with us children.

The chauffeur was Berry, and the groom was Charles. We especially loved to go to the beautifully kept stables to pat my eldest uncle's hunters, which were kept there because he was serving in the army in India, at the time. On Sundays there was a family ritual in which we all took part, trooping round to the stables after church to give the rather grand and disdainful hunters their carrots and sugar lumps. For the grandchildren there was a delightfully woolly white donkey called Snowdrop, on which we used to ride.

In the kitchen Emily, the cook, held sway, with her stocky red-haired kitchen maid, Agnes. There was a small weedy youth called Sidney who had to help Emily by lifting down her huge pots and pans and scrubbing them after use. I think he also cleaned the knives (which were steel bladed), and the shoes, of which there must have been very large numbers. Grannie had a decidedly socialist streak in her character and, in spite of her ability to make such a luxurious home for her husband's family, she secretly felt rather guilty about it all. This was evident in the way she was affected by the thought of employing the poor little scullery boy. She could not bear to think of his life below stairs, heaving heavy pots and pans and being given all the dirtiest jobs to do, and she promptly sent him into the Navy.

Emily would then insist on having another boy in his place and exactly the same thing would happen all over again. I suspect that poor Emily must have been distraught, but it relieved Grannie's troubled conscience to know that she had released several young men from servility. I never heard whether any of her kitchen boys ever rose to the rank of Admiral, though.

Grannie must have been a very exceptional woman with a good grasp of politics, although she was far too good a wife and mother ever to think of working openly for the rights of women. But she was a District Councillor, and she was always full of very advanced ideas for world peace, including (as early as the 1930's) her pet theory that the European countries and Britain should join together in a "common market". Knowing that her Danish grandfather's country of Schleswig Holstein had been acquired by Germany after being tossed around like a political football, it is not surprising that Grannie was a dedicated European, long before most people had even begun to think of such a concept. Grannie had a very thorough knowledge of European history, which she taught to her daughters, who were, all three, educated at home to a very high standard. There was only one language which they refused to learn and that was German. The anti-German feeling was already strong by the time my mother started her school lessons, the First World War having been declared shortly after her thirteenth birthday.

Grannie was musical, somehow always seeming to know the right person to bring to Hitcham to teach her daughters their three chosen musical instruments; piano, violin and cello. My mother's eldest sister, Bridget (known as Betty), was taught the violin by the composer Frank Bridge, and when he realised that the Hanbury girls were musical, he composed his now well-known "Miniatures" for them and dedicated the pieces to "Betty and Rachel". My mother was a particularly talented young pianist, and went on to be taught by Alicia Brecht, a sister of Mathilde Verne, who had taught the child prodigy, Solomon.

Grannie loved to see her large family enjoying themselves, and I can remember life at Hitcham as being full of fun. We acted charades and plays for the grown-ups, we played silly games with them after tea – like animal grab, and puff billiards, or riotous games of Racing Demon. Sometimes we turned out all the lights and played "Murder", but that was stopped when my cousin John broke Grannie's best Sevres vase, bumping into it in the dark. Best of all, our parents formed a jazz band; even their husbands were musical – I believe they would not have been allowed by Grannie to marry our mothers unless they had been!

Uncle Fitz (married to our favourite aunt, Rachel, known to us all as Aunt "Woggie") played the banjo and ukelele almost as well as George Formby. My father played the fiddle and my mother the piano. I suppose Auntie Woggie must have played her cello or perhaps, the double bass.

They played Scott Joplin and all the old favourites; "Smoke Gets in Your Eyes", "Dancing Cheek to Cheek", and "The Charleston"; and we children danced our own impromptu steps on the beautifully polished floors in time to the music. When I got too hot from bouncing up and down, I used to go to the front hall and lean up against the lovely cool classical marble group of a man, a woman and a child, which we irreverently called "Adam and Eve and Pinch-me". Sometimes the gaiety and the noise became almost too much for a five-year-old and I would retreat to the outer hall where the Hall-boy's hooded leather chair stood, and curl up inside it, as though I was in a tent. It was peaceful there and I could think my own thoughts.

Because Grannie's two sons and three sons-in-law were all in the Army or the Navy, she was used to providing a refuge for them, and for her grandchildren, at Hitcham, when they returned from postings abroad, or when they had to move house. In the early 1930's neither of the Hanbury sons, my mother's two brothers, were married, but the three daughters (two married to sailors, and one to a soldier) had produced two children each. Strangely, three of their babies were all born within three months of each other, and they were all boys. As a result, my brother Robin and my two cousins, Bill and John, were all the same age, and were known as "The Three Musketeers'.

My mother's eldest sister, Betty, was tragically killed in a hunting accident in Jersey, where she had gone to live on her marriage to Kit Riley (of the Coldstream Guards). Her two children were only seven and four when she died, so these two grandchildren used to spend even more time at Hitcham than the rest of us.

All the cousins were at Hitcham when we arrived home from South Africa, including the two oldest, Bill's older brother, Nicholas, and John's elder sister, who had been given the unusual name of Andalusia, so we called her "Andie'; sadly both Nick and Andie were much too old to play with me, but Bill and John decided I wasn't too bad, as girls go, and allowed me to join in most of their games, with Robin. The "Three Musketeers" were shortly to go to their prep schools, for all three were approaching their eighth birthdays during that summer of 1933.

I can remember Nanny sewing on name tapes, and helping to pack their school trunks and tuck-boxes, while we played happily in the rambling gardens. There was one large level area of grass on which my grandparents had thoughtfully created a play-area, first for their own children, and subsequently for us, the next generation, with swings, a see-saw, a little wooden switch-back "railway" with a trolley which ran up and down under its own momentum after being launched from its highest point; and, best of all, the "giant-stride".

I have never seen a "giant-stride" anywhere else to this day, although I have seen photographs in a book showing the ill-fated children of the Russian royal family playing on one, in the gardens of their palace in St. Petersburg. It is like a maypole with ropes hanging from a swivel and wooden handles at the bottom of the ropes. Each child grasped one of these handles and started to run round in an ever-widening circle until their feet lifted off the ground and they flew through the air, screaming with joy as they whirled round. It only worked properly if there were three or four children, so it was perfect for John, Bill, Robin and me and we had endless fun on it.

The boys all had bicycles by now and I remember how they did the most terrifying things on them. The most exciting and daring trick of all was to bicycle up the narrow plank of the huge see-saw and (trying not to fall off as you caught the point of balance with a bump) you free-wheeled down the other side to the safety of the ground. I used to watch my dare-devil brother and cousins with my heart in my mouth, filled with admiration for their bravery.

I took my affection for my brother totally for granted at that age, but this new emotion, for two first cousins, was quite different and very special. Bill was the funny one who always made me laugh, and John was the one who was kindest to me. I can remember persuading John to be my pet monkey in a

SAILOR'S DAUGHTER

private game I was playing, and he patiently hopped about attached to a piece of string tied to the buttonhole of his strap shoe, performing tricks for me, which he must have found decidedly boring, but he never complained.

My grandfather presented the grandchildren with a beautiful rowing boat to use on the pond at the foot of the long grassy slope to the south-east of the house. We had a launching ceremony, and, being the youngest, I was allowed to pronounce the name of the boat, "*H.M.S. Ali Baba*", I declaimed loudly, adding, in true Naval fashion, "God bless this ship and all who sail in her". We then all piled in and rowed a lap of honour round the pond, with the grown-ups cheering on the bank.

Grandfather was still busy with his family hop business in those days, and he was also a director of the Bank of England and chairman of the Guardian Assurance Company. He was a very quiet, lovable and unassuming man, small in stature and especially good with children. One day, soon after our return from Africa, he asked me who had taught me to talk (I had only been a baby when I left) and I replied, "No-one, God of course".

None of us were aware of his distinguished business career, and all I can ever remember being told was that he was "something in the City". Every day he departed for London by train from Taplow Station with a rose in his buttonhole. Nanny and I used to sing "Every Monday morning, when I go up to London, I see the little puff puffs lined up in a row – the man inside the engine pulls a little lever – Chuff chuff – Whee! Whee! Off we go!" This song was always to be associated in my mind with Grandfather's daily departure for London. At this point I had no idea how much my life was going to change before the end of the year. Neither did I know that, quite soon, I, too, was to go on a train, on a long journey with the entire household from Hitcham.

# CHAPTER IV

＊

EVEN NAVAL FAMILIES spent long periods of their lives away from the sea. Just before 12th August 1933, I remember a huge and exciting upheaval. My grandfather took us all to Scotland. And when I say all, I do literally mean all. Not only my grandparents, my uncles and aunts and cousins, but also Massey and Berry, Bertram, Emily, Agnes, Sidney, and Charles, the butler, footman, cook, kitchen maid, scullery boy, the groom and the chauffeur. The notable exception for me was to be Nanny who, although she was coming briefly to Scotland to settle me in, was then going away for her first long holiday since she came to our family in 1925. I was far too excited about going to Scotland to think that I might miss Nanny when she went away.

We were going to Lendrick Lodge, near Callander, in Perthshire – rented annually by my grandfather from the Earl of Moray – for the shooting and stalking. To transport this huge family, my grandfather booked a complete railway carriage into which we all piled at Taplow Station. Dancing with excitement on the platform, I watched the luggage being loaded in: the guns and rifles, packing cases of linen and silver, provisions, ammunition and, finally, our suitcases, followed by the gun dogs who were my special friends. We were then distributed throughout the compartments; Nanny, Emily, Agnes and I shared a four-berth one. In those days the sleeping berths were covered with a rather prickly moquette, and the only additions to comfort for the night were a pillow and a grey tickly blanket. This was my first experience of this form of overnight travel; I was ultimately to find myself doing it six times a year, from my Scottish home to my boarding-school in England (in an ordinary sleeping compartment which I shared each time with three complete strangers), after we had gone to live permanently on the Clyde during the Second World War. I also got to know the Glasgow railway station extremely well, in due course.

At Taplow our private coach was attached to the Great Western Railway (G.W.R.) train from Taplow up to London. In London there was always a tremendous amount of huffing and puffing and hooting and bumping, as we were uncoupled and moved across endless points by a small shunting engine, till we had been attached to the overnight train to Perth, which would travel on the London & North Western Railway, by the west coast route, over the high ground at Shap, down the long hill to Penrith and Carlisle, and from there into Scotland.

As far as I can remember, we were allowed to stay up until the carriage was safely attached to the night train to Scotland, so that we could watch all the fun. It was an exciting, if noisy and dirty experience, with clouds of steam, smuts and sparks flying in all directions like an inferno; jolts and crashes and bangs, and sudden petulant hooting on a very high-pitched note, quite unlike the satisfactory baritone roar that our ocean liner used to make, or the whooping of the *Cardiff*.

The boys were particularly enchanted by the steam engines, as are all small boys (and bigger ones, too!). For my own part, I found the shunting rather alarming and tedious, and longed for the train to get going on its journey to Scotland. Meanwhile, I removed myself to the rear portion of the long carriage to sit amongst the luggage, between the two black labradors, Nell and Dusk, holding their paws for mutual comfort. The poor dogs were finding all the strange noises just as disconcerting as I did.

Eventually, we were off, I sprang up on to my top bunk and Nanny helped to roll me in my blanket. I remember we slept in our clothes, Nanny being highly suspicious of the cleanliness of the thick grey blankets. I also remember that I hardly slept a wink all night. It was partly the excitement, partly the noise, and partly the unfamiliar movement of the train – the first I could remember I had ever been in. But it was also to a large extent Emily's tummy which rumbled ceaselessly all night. I could have got used to the rumbling itself, but every time it rumbled, Emily felt obliged to say, "Pardon me!", very loudly, which made sleep impossible.

Later generations brought up on television versions of the hierarchy of the big house (such as in "Upstairs, Downstairs") may be surprised that Nanny and I were sharing our compartment with the cook and the kitchen-maid – but this was a perfectly natural state of affairs in my young days. I probably felt far more at ease in their company than with the grown-ups, who expected impossible standards of behaviour at all times, and still preferred children to be "seen and not heard".

Being with Emily and Agnes was far more fun, and far more relaxing for us all (admittedly, they called me "Miss Jean" – and still do to this day, even though I, myself, am now a grandmother; Emily having recently celebrated her hundredth birthday, while Agnes is widowed and living in a Yorkshire village). Another mistake of television (a rare one because their research nowadays is impeccable) is when one of the characters refers to "Cook". We invariably called the servants by their names and it was considered decidedly bad manners to talk about "Cook" or "Nurse" (for Nanny). At Hitcham my grandmother's servants were very real friends to us all, and I feel sure that they were considerately treated by the whole family. They certainly never seemed to want to leave, and had just as much fun in the servants' hall as we had in the drawing-room, judging by the noise and laughter I used to hear, and occasionally be allowed to join in, behind the green baize door.

Lendrick Lodge was set on the edge of the Trossachs, beside Loch Vennachar and beneath Ben Ledi. It was a child's paradise. The house was grey with painted wooden eaves, and of an irregular shape, which a child always finds irresistible.

Looking at it from outside I could never quite make out in which protuberance my bedroom window was situated. It was very similar to many other Victorian shooting lodges scattered over the Highlands, all built shortly after Queen Victoria and Prince Albert made it fashionable to go to Scotland for the shooting. This new fashion became fun for the prosperous gentry, but not much fun for the displaced crofters who had been sent to America, having been told that grouse and deer were now a far better economic proposition for the landlords than crofting and sheep.

Fortunately, for my peace of mind as a child, this state of affairs was not much discussed, and I continued to enjoy myself in blissful ignorance that harsh sacrifices had been made so that wealthy businessmen like my grandfather could enjoy their sport in Scotland in the 1920's and 1930's.

Certainly my grandfather was a particularly kind man who would have been very upset if his own employees or tenants were to suffer in any way, but as the clearances had taken place nearly three generations ago, he could not have felt personally responsible. As the tenant, he was only concerned with taking his family for an enjoyable holiday in the Highlands, just as King George V and Queen Mary now did, every year. The removal of the crofters from their homes in the nineteenth century was a sad fact of history, and could not be reversed even by the most enlightened and liberal of landowners or tenants in the 1930's. There was too, a grain of comfort in the fact that some of the Scots who had survived the appalling crossing of the Atlantic had carved a far more prosperous life for themselves and their families in the New World, than would ever have been possible on the inhospitable moorlands or wetlands of the Scottish Highlands.

Nanny went off for her holiday soon after we arrived at Lendrick Lodge, and I was put into the care of Andie's and John's Swiss governess, Elsa, who looked exactly like a slightly plumper version of Julie Andrews in "The Sound of Music", and treated me and my cousins in a very similar way to the Von Trapp children, with lots of singing and laughter and plenty of energetic walks up Ben Ledi, which rose to nearly 3,000 feet to the top. We grew visibly stronger and pinker, and all enjoyed ourselves a great deal.

Children have always loved playing at soldiers and it was almost as though we had a premonition that within five or six years we should be at war when we formed ourselves into a "private army". We were provided with wooden swords, made by the four boys, with which we were drilled by thirteen-year-old Nicholas who was about to become a Naval cadet, having been accepted by the Royal Naval College at Dartmouth.

Being only five-years-old, I was extremely flattered to be allowed to join this army. I was three years younger than "the three musketeers", and was determined to keep up with the best of them. This was quite a struggle, as my legs were a great deal shorter and fatter than their's, but my determination won the day, and when Nicholas told me that I was "a good sport", I basked in a glow of self-importance. Our best battles took place in a sheep fank (the Perthshire word for a sheep-fold) on the lower slopes of Ben Ledi. We reached the fank by a path which started up the hill immediately behind the house.

As far as I can remember, we were all on the same side, defending our fort (the sheep fank) from an imaginary enemy. Being further up the hillside, we had a distinct advantage over our enemy. Like children to this day, we made the appropriate shooting noises, "pow! pee-ew! wham! wroomph!", as the battle raged thick and fast. I had been relegated to the position of Red-Cross nurse, and had great fun tying my cousins up in bandages made out of old rags we had pinched from the housemaids' cupboard. Like my shoelaces, the knots I tied were impossible to undo, so, at the end of the battle, everyone trooped home to tea looking like the occupants of a military hospital. The only other girl in our army was my red-headed cousin Andie, who was going through a tomboy stage at twelve-years-old, and wore grey flannel shorts like the boys. She much preferred being in the "front line", and left all the "nursing" to me, which I thoroughly enjoyed.

Towards the end of the holidays, we discovered a much more satisfactory weapon than our wooden swords. If our parents, or Elsa, had realised what we were up to, they would have put a stop to it at once. The boys had been given "tips" by some of my grandfather's male shooting guests, as was the custom in those days. In Callander, on a family shopping expedition, they bought us each a pea-shooter. Next to the toy-shop was the sweetie shop, so the boys took the precaution of spending their remaining cash on Edinburgh Rock, to account for their shopping activities. Pea-shooters were definitely prohibited by the grown-ups, just as we were never allowed chewing-gum. So naturally, these were the two things we always longed to buy.

When we got home, with the pea-shooters successfully concealed, we had to decide on our ammunition. We could not use peas because we'd have to ask Emily for them; so we decided on rowan-berries. At first we climbed up the hill again and fired them at our imaginary enemy from the sheep fank – but that soon began to get boring, and one of the boys suggested it would be far more fun to hide beside the main road, and fire at the passing tourist traffic on its way to the Trossachs.

The ensuing hour was one of the most satisfactory I can ever remember. Pea-shooters are very accurate weapons (you put them to your lips and blow hard, pointing them towards your victim), and we had great fun directing our fairly harmless rowan berries at cars, as they sped past. Sometimes the occupants must have heard the sharp ping on the bodywork of their car, and we fell about laughing behind our hedge, as we saw the looks of surprise as they turned their heads to see where the strange sounds came from. But like so many children's games, it finally all ended in tears. Well, not exactly tears, but with six very chastened and somewhat alarmed children. One of the rowan berries hit a motor-cyclist full in the face (in those days they did not wear space helmets and their bikes went much slower) and although he was quite unhurt, it gave him such a fright that he leapt off his bike and came to look for his assailants. He soon found us lurking behind the hedge, trembling with fear, and told us that he was going straight off to inform the police.

For the rest of that afternoon, we waited in a state of terrified apprehension for the local policeman to arrive on his bicycle and for all to be revealed. But nothing ever happened. Whether the motor-cyclist had only issued a threat, or whether, when he went to the police they had telephoned my grandfather, who had probably laughed it off, explaining it was just a childish prank in which no-one had actually been hurt, we were never to know. Never again did we fire rowan-berries at passing motorists – we had learnt a useful lesson. It is also a possibility that, because Grandfather was a good customer in the local town and provided employment for the keepers, the police may have decided to ignore the incident. For our own part, we were far too alarmed to try the same game again.

After this our private army was voluntarily disbanded and we spent the rest of the time "messing about in boats" on Loch Vennachar, and making piers out of the large stones which lay beside the loch. We had all learnt to row and to manoeuvre a boat, just like the children in Swallows and Amazons, but we did not sail. The sudden gusts of wind from the surrounding hills made sailing too dangerous, and the loch was several miles long and very deep. We just messed about at the shallow end of the loch, nearest to Lendrick, where there were sandy beaches and reed beds and a great many moorhens, wild ducks – and even some hissing swans of which we kept well clear.

The cook, Emily, had a daughter called Freda, a fat little girl, a year or two older than me; and Grannie, with characteristic thoughtfulness, had invited her to spend part of her holidays at Lendrick with her mother. Freda and I developed a close friendship and enjoyed looking for wild flowers and unusual pebbles on the loch's shore together, while the older ones took part in mock sea-battles in the rowing boats.

Then, one day, Grandfather bought us the most exciting toy of all, called a Flexi-Racer. It was a sort of toboggan on wheels, a sophisticated version of the Scots' street child's "carty", but this one had a steering system and brakes. Grannie was horrified at first, as were my mother and Auntie Woggie, but as far as I can remember, nobody suffered any great injury, and we took turns on the back drive, shooting down a hill with the same delicious and hair-raising sensations as those of being on a roller-coaster. The great speeds we reached were too glorious for words.

The sporting activities at Lendrick were mainly for the benefit of the grown-ups. Children did not often join in adult pursuits with their parents in those days, and were kept segregated to a certain extent in case they were a nuisance, or made too much noise. But, sometimes, we climbed the hill behind the house with Charles, the groom, and the pony laden with panniers of food, to join in the shooting lunch with our parents and grandparents. I was usually allowed to ride the fat pony up the hill, with my bottom wedged between the panniers and my legs sticking straight out on either side. The lunch was a delicious and substantial picnic provided by Emily. Usually cold grouse and baps, followed by jam puffs (her flaky pastry melted in the mouth) and thickly buttered gingerbread. The grown-ups often had biscuits and stilton cheese as well, but children were not often allowed cheese in those days – it was considered to be a delicacy (like caviar or smoked salmon), and far too indigestible for us – also, we used to be told, it would probably give us nightmares. I had plenty of nightmares already, so was quite happy to go without it.

We ate our lunch sprawled on tartan rugs in the heather amongst the grown-ups, who carried on their own intriguing chatter and seldom brought us into the conversation, as was the way of things in those days. Occasionally, when the gossip got really juicy, someone would remember us and say "Pas devant les enfants". As we all understood French, we were even more intrigued. To keep our bottoms from getting damp, in case there wasn't enough rug to go round, we had each been provided with a small folding water-proof square to sit on, which were known in our family as "jeely-pieces". The final treat at the end of lunch was when Grannie offered round a tin of "Hawick Balls", which were delicious brown peppermint humbugs. Little did I then realise that I was to spend the second half of my life near Hawick, where they are made to this day.

Sometimes we stayed on after lunch for the first grouse-drive. I had always been frightened of bangs (particularly since my recent alarming South African experience) and secretly hoped that I should be allowed, instead, to ride the pony home with Charles. But, if there had been a particularly large bag before lunch, then the grouse went back with the pony, and there was no room for me.

I used to sit in the bottom of my father's butt with my fingers in my ears, praying that the beaters would fail to raise any birds. Sometimes a lone grouse in front of the butt would chuckle "Go back! Go back!". I heartily agreed and hoped its friends were listening. I think my father understood my agony, but his theory was that we had to "get used to" the things we didn't like, or were frightened of. Strangely enough, my objection to shooting had nothing to do with killing the birds. I did not mind that part of it at all, and I positively loved the smell of game, and of gunpowder. It was the loudness and suddenness of the bang that terrified me.

Recently, I found myself in total sympathy with a four-year-old grandson who saw that his father was about to open a bottle of wine for lunch, in honour of our visit, and promptly put his fingers in his ears. Everyone looked rather surprised, but I knew exactly what was worrying him, "It's all right darling", I whispered to him, "it's not champagne. This cork isn't going to go bang!" (We had drunk champagne at his younger brother's christening a few months earlier.) Even then, he kept his fingers in his ears until the cork was drawn, just in case his grandmother had been misled.

Sometimes, instead of grouse-driving, my father and mother would go deer-stalking. My mother was probably the better rifle shot of the two, and they both kept a tally of the stags they had shot with notches on their walking sticks. They always brought me back some sprigs of white heather from these expeditions and, if they had been successful, I used to be allowed to watch the stag arriving back, slung across the hill pony's special saddle, and being weighed and hung up in the game larder – which was a little building separate from the house, with slatted vents and huge hooks hanging from the ceiling.

The strong smell of stag was permanently associated with the game larder. It was not an unpleasant smell, and I can only describe it as an extraordinarily "virile" smell, exuding strength, and a primaeval wildness of spirit. Even a small child can feel these strong connections often associated with a particular smell.

On one triumphant occasion, my father brought back a "Royal" – a stag with twelve points to its antlers. If one had been spied on the hill, the stalker only allowed "his gentleman" to kill it if he had never had a "Royal" before. Most of the stags that were killed by my grandfather's party were the ones that were "going back", or had some defect. Deer-stalking is a part of the hunter's art and beasts are never killed purely to satisfy the marksman's pride. Hunting and deer-stalking are the same as culling, which is a way of helping to keep the natural environmental balance. This had all been explained to me many times, which was probably why I was quite unmoved by dead animals. Basically, I also knew that they were mainly shot "for the pot". Emily used to give us superb roast venison, accompanied by red currant jelly, in a thick gravy laced with Madeira, for Sunday lunch at Lendrick. My mother knew that food was my real weakness, and used to embarrass me by telling visitors to Lendrick that, at about the age of two, I had once seen a very sweet rabbit sitting up in our garden washing his face with his paws, and had remarked, "Quick! Quick! Toot him for my dinner!".

I suppose I must have been missing Nanny's attentions a good deal at that time, so my mother sometimes took me off for walks alone. We used to go to a place we both loved, called the Drum. It was a strange little fairy hill between the house and the loch, covered with small gnarled trees, and with thick green moss and blaeberries underfoot. Growing amongst the blaeberries under the tiny trees were the delicate mauve harebells (mauve was still my favourite colour, since my *Cardiff* birthday cake), and in the moss we found red and white spotted toadstools, which my mother called "Rogie-stools". When I was very small, my father used to take me on his knees and sing a song about "rogies" which he had made up:

> "With a laugh and a shout the rogies came out,
>   The rogies came out, the rogies came out,
>   In their beetleskin boots and sealskin capes,
>   Of various shapes of various shapes . . .
>   Sssh! . . . all the rogies came out!"

At which point he would tickle me all over until I screamed with delight. This song has continued to delight two more generations of babies since then!

My mother and I used to make fairy houses together out of moss and wild flowers when we were alone on the Drum. She told me that she had first made them as a child with an old friend called Daisy Wardrop, of whom she was very fond. Daisy Wardrop lived in Musselburgh, and was yet another Scottish link for me. She was my godmother and she used to write me delightful letters in her spikey "Edwardian" writing. Although we hardly ever met, I always thought of her as someone very special.

The Drum was such a peaceful, quiet place, and I think my mother liked to use me as an excuse to escape from the crowd at The Lodge. Like me, she, too, enjoyed being alone, and she told me that she once remembered standing beside my grandmother, as a little girl, looking at a beautiful sunrise and saying, "Wouldn't it be lovely if there were no peoples in the world?". On other occasions we used to go and fish for trout together in a small burn near the house, with a wriggling worm on the end of a hook, another pleasantly solitary and peaceful ploy.

1.

2.

3.

4.

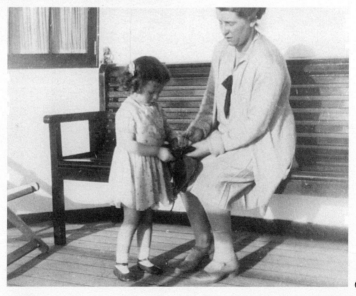

6.

8.

9.

10.

11.

13.

16.

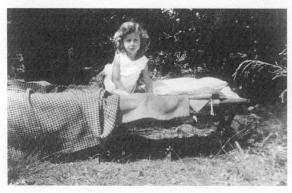

17.

18.

24.

25.

26.

27.

28.

29.

30.

31.

32.

33.

34.

35.

36.

37.

39.

40.

41.

42.

44.

46.

47.

48.

50.

1.

52.

53.

56.

57.

58.

59.

61.

63.

64.

65.

66.

67.

68.

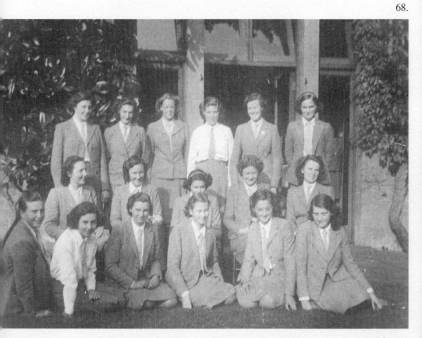

69.

71.

72.

73.

74.

# TITLES OF ILLUSTRATIONS

1   Angus Cunninghame Graham.
2   Nanny, with Jean at six months.
3   Patricia Cunninghame Graham, with Robin, aged 4, and Jean, aged nine months.
4   Patricia, with Jean, at Hitcham.
5   Angus and Patricia at the Garth Hunt Meet.
6   On deck with nanny.
7   Jean's second birthday (flowers from the maids).
8   Robin and Jean.
9   My "bike" (third birthday present).
10  The Boulders, our home in South Africa.
11  On board SS *Dunbar Castle,* bound for South Africa, 1931.
12  *Cardiff* Boys to tea (from HMS *Arethusa*).
13  Samson – Zulu cook.
14  Jean, with Gertrude ("Rosebud").
15  Fourth birthday – wearing green socks.
16  Playing on the beach, in "poke bonnets".
17  A mid-day nap, on a camping expedition.
18  HMS *Cardiff.*
19  Robin going aboard HMS *Cardiff* at Simonstown for the trip home to England.
20  Admiral Teddy Evans (C-in-C, Simonstown) and Patricia.
21  Angus in full dress uniform.
22  The "Welcome Home" party at Hitcham.
23  Cousins at Hitcham.
24  Lendrick Lodge, Callander, Perthshire.
25  The Hanbury "household" at Lendrick.
26  "Private army" (Jean, Robin, John, Bill, "Andie", Nick).
27  "Private army" on Ben Ledi.

54 At Fanling, going to the stables to ride our ponies (New Territories, China).

55 Angus Cunninghame Graham and his gunboat HMS *Tarantula,* at Canton.

56 On the bridge of HMS *Tarantula* (S.N.O., West River, China).

57 Back at Ardoch, John, Andie and Bill, spending their holidays with us.

58 Haccombe House (near Newton Abbot) – Rookesbury Park School evacuated there during the Second World War.

59 A hard frost on the Lake of Menteith (Bill, Jean, Patricia and Robin).

60 Father and Robert – Captain and Cadet.

61 The Signal School, Portsmouth – a visit from King George VI when A.C.G. was the Captain during the Second World War.

62 Jean and Rogie.

63 The Taylors, our evacuees from Clydebank, at Ardoch.

64 HMS *Kent.*

65 "A near miss."

66 The Commander of HMS *Kent,* George Oswald, on leave, with his sons Julian (who became First Sea Lord 1989–93) and David.

67 Father (A.C.G.) on the bridge of HMS *Kent.*

68 "The Class of 1941–45", at St. Mary's School, Calne (the sixth form).

69 "The Gods of Olympus" – a frolic by the sixth form at St. Mary's.

70 The Chopin ballet at St. Mary's.

71 Father is now an Admiral – with his friends, Sir Philip Vian and Freddie Dalrymple Hamilton, 1946.

72 Admiral Sir Angus Cunninghame Graham (after 40 years' service in the Royal Navy), second-in-command of the Home Fleet, 1946.

73 Jean, as a debutante, going to the first Queen Charlotte's Ball after the Second World War, in 1946.

74 Jean Cunninghame Graham – Lady Polwarth – at Harden, Hawick, 1986.

# CHAPTER V

WE HAD NOW BEEN staying with my grandparents, first at Hitcham, and then at Lendrick, for more than three months. But my father was still waiting for news of his next Naval appointment. While we were at Lendrick we heard that he was to attend the R.A.F. Staff College at Andover in the New Year – his third Staff College appointment. He knew that he was unlikely to be given another sea command so soon after his exceptional posting as the Commander of the *Cardiff* in South Africa.

When we left Lendrick, life was to change more than I could have believed possible. I soon discovered that my beloved Nanny had not merely "gone away for a holiday", but had left us for good, and had gone to Kent to look after a new baby. I was inconsolable.

I suppose my mother must have given me an explanation for her departure at the time, but I don't remember what it was. As I grew older I came to realise that my mother had found Nanny "difficult". This was a huge surprise to me, for I could not believe that my mother could possibly have failed to get on with Nanny, whom I loved almost more than anyone else in the world, and with whom I always felt totally safe, and deeply loved in return. Nowadays, mothers give far more time to their children than was normal when I was small, so we depended greatly on the love given so freely by our nannies, who were nearly always childless themselves.

I remember Nanny's departure was followed, for me, by a very unhappy winter. Not only did I miss her badly, but I reacted to the change of climate by developing a series of very bad colds, and sore throats. I was so stuffed up that I could hardly breathe. I dreaded the nasty medicine I had to take, which seemed to do no good. Worse still, I used to have my throat "painted", which was a barbarous cure for sore throats, with a long quill paintbrush dipped in a very strong antiseptic, literally painted on the inside of the throat, the patient "gagging" the while.

I spent a great deal of time in bed, at Hitcham, when we got back from Lendrick. My father was taking part in various courses at this time, so Hitcham was still our temporary home, although he was away a good deal. Elsa, the Swiss nursery governess, had now come to look after me permanently in Nanny's place, and Robin had gone away to school.

My mother decided to cheer me up, by letting me have my heart's desire – and a very small wire-haired terrier puppy arrived at Hitcham, in a basket. I was ecstatic, and promptly named him "Rogie".

Tragically, the puppy must have arrived with the distemper virus on him, and within a few days he died, being too young to stand up to the illness. This was yet another cause for heartbreak, and I can remember lying in bed, stuffed up with cold, crying myself to sleep. Nanny had left, Robin had gone away to school, and now the dear little puppy I had so longed for, had died. Life was hardly worth living, and I wished that I was back in South Africa where I had been so happy.

After Nanny left, I was moved from the nursery wing, to sleep in the dressing-room attached to my parent's huge and comfortable bedroom, which had windows looking across to a distant view of Windsor Castle. The view was superbly romantic for a small child and it must have been this that brought my "imaginary family" into being. There was also, in my bedroom, one of those screens covered with pictures of old-fashioned scenes from Christmas cards, gaudy flowers from bulb catalogues and colourful pictures cut from magazines, which served as yet another stimulation to my already vivid imagination.

As soon as I was tucked into bed (with a fire flickering in a small black grate in my bedroom, in an attempt to prevent me from catching yet another cold), my "family" used to come "alive". They came from the sixteenth century, in the days of Good Queen Bess, and they wore exquisite clothes. The eldest of this large high-spirited family of children, was about the same age as my oldest cousin, Nicholas. But they were definitely not replicas of my cousins – they were an entirely different family, with their own individual looks and characters. I used to lie in bed thinking about them, in a happy drowsy state going over their names, and choosing what they should wear out of their extensive Elizabethan wardrobes. I can still remember the boys in their colourful doublets and hose, and the girls in tight-fitting long brocade dresses with white linen ruffs round their necks, and bright satin slippers on their feet. My favourite little girl had long fair hair, and I gave her the name Miriam. She was a year or two younger than me, perhaps about four-years-old. I used to have long conversations with them all. How strange to find, in time, that the writer Elizabeth Goudge had a similar family, and that she put them into her enchanting book about sixteenth-century Oxford, *Towers in the Mist*.

If Hitcham had been an old Elizabethan manor house, I might have been tempted to think of them as ghosts, for they seemed perfectly real to me. There had, in fact, once been an Elizabethan house on the site, before my great-grandfather built his own mansion. But it had not occupied the same piece of ground, it had stood in what we called "the Old Garden", across the other side of the road to Burnham. This was a beautiful walled garden with brick paths, bright with polyanthus, scented with rosemary and lavender, and in the summer, purple irises, pergolas of trailing wisteria and roses, and clumps of herbaceous and perennial sweet smelling flowers in the borders.

There was a water tank in the Elizabethan garden in which lived a newt. Beside the large goldfish pond was an old tin full of square dog biscuits and a mallet with which we could crush the biscuit and feed the crumbs to the goldfish. I thought the dog biscuits were quite delicious, and used to eat them surreptitiously, when no-one was looking.

The explanation for my imaginary family was really quite simple: they were the result of my fertile imagination, combined with my current fit of loneliness since Nanny left and the puppy died, and after such a glorious summer spent in the company of my amusing and attractive cousins.

There was another unpleasant memory that winter when my Uncle Fitz went down with a dangerous attack of measles. He was very ill and nurses were summoned to look after him. To prevent any of the children from catching measles, a huge sheet dipped in carbolic was hung across the passage that led to his room, which I found alarmingly sinister. Fortunately, he soon recovered, the sheet was removed to my great relief, and the nurses departed.

Then, Robin, who had also been having incessant sore throats during his first term at prep school, came home to have his tonsils removed in a nursing home in Windsor. I remember visiting him the day after the operation and being astonished to hear him speaking in a tiny squeaky voice because his throat hurt so much. He was given ice-cream to eat, which I shared, and in return I gave him my most treasured possession, a paper parachute which had arrived with my comic, *Tiger Tim*. This was a great act of self-sacrifice on my part, as I thought the little pink paper parachute was one of the most intriguing playthings I had ever had. To make up for my generosity to my brother, Elsa took me to tea at Fuller's in the High Street at Windsor, where we ate chocolate cake. She also bought me a packet of lollipops, which were all colours of the rainbow and not only delicious to suck but beautiful to look at, as well.

By Christmas all our miseries were over, and Hitcham came to life again as the family began to assemble once more. Christmas Eve was my grandfather's birthday, and for tea we had his birthday cake covered with shimmering candles. We also had "snapdragon" – sultanas and raisins in a dish of flaming brandy, the game being to see how many you were brave enough to pick out of the flames.

After tea, everyone rushed upstairs to wrap up their Christmas presents. As I was wandering upstairs in a happy dream, I suddenly heard one of the grown-ups call out,

"Quick, come and look at the camels!"

I rushed to the nearest window to peer out into the darkness expecting to see the three kings come riding up to the front door. Instead, I saw a huddle of small boys in scarves and caps holding lanterns, who started to sing,

"God rest you merry gentlemen
    let nothing you dismay . . ."

The stars were twinkling and their feet were crunching on the frosty gravel. "But mummy, where are the camels?" I demanded. My mother burst out laughing as she hurried to open the front door to welcome the boys into the hall. "Not camels, silly! Carols! It's the church choir – they come every year!".

That night I had another disappointment – I had hung up my stocking at the end of the bed, and was trying hard to get to sleep because I knew Father Christmas only came after you were asleep. I felt much too excited to sleep. Massey sounded the "changing gong" in the hall with several loud "boom-booms". Half an hour later, I heard the gong for dinner. The grown-ups went clattering down the polished staircase, and then the hum of their cheerful voices and their bursts of laughter, sounds of glasses and knives and forks went on interminably. I still couldn't go to sleep. Later, I heard my father's violin, and my mother singing "How beautiful they are, the lordly ones", and "I'll follow my secret heart", two of her favourite songs. Shortly after that I must have fallen into a light doze, to be awakened by the sound of my door opening gently, followed by the rustling of paper, and other sounds which were undoubtedly my stocking being filled. Father Christmas had come! I must not let him see that I was still half awake or he might go away again. I shut my eyes tight, but he went on pushing parcels into my stocking and I just had to peep at him once. Only once. Yes, it was him, he had on his red cloak, just as I'd expected, and he was bending over so that I could not see his face or beard, tying the final balloon to my bedpost.

Then I heard my father's whisper, "I've finished doing Robin's one. Are you nearly done?" and his head came round my door. Father Christmas looked up. "Ssh! Just coming!" It was my mother's voice and then I recognised her red velvet dress and could smell her scent. I shut my eyes even tighter as she came round the bed and planted a kiss on my forehead. "Sound asleep!" she whispered to my father, "doesn't she look sweet?" and they left the room.

I didn't feel at all sweet, I was absolutely furious. What had happened to Father Christmas? Why had he sent my mother to fill my stocking instead? It was the most dreadful disappointment. Then it dawned on me: he didn't exist after all. My mother and father had been pretending about him all along. It was a terrible shock, and I felt very let down. My mother had no business to be wearing a red velvet dress and raising my hopes like that. Before I could make up my mind to investigate further, I had fallen fast asleep.

Next morning, Robin and I jumped into our parents' bed to open our stockings. I did not even mention the revelation of the previous night, and when my mother and father made reference to the reindeers' bells they had heard during the night, I went along with the pretence, looking suitably intrigued. I had soon forgotten my disappointment. The contents of my stocking was far too exciting, right down to the tangerine in the toe.

We had woken very early, as all children do on Christmas morning, so, to keep us quiet until it was time to get up, my father said he would tell us a story – "Tell us about Jutland again!" we both exclaimed. My father had been a young lieutenant in H.M.S. *Agincourt* at the Battle of Jutland and his eye-witness account of one of the last great sea battles in the First World War fascinated us. He told us that his ship had been built on the Tyne for the Brazilians, and then sold to the Turks, as the *Sultan Osman I*. But, while waiting in the Tyne for her Turkish crew to arrive, Winston Churchill, as First Lord of the Admiralty, had decided to acquire the ship for the Royal Navy instead, because of her huge armament of 44 guns. The Turks never forgave him, and this was almost certainly one of the reasons that brought Turkey into the First World War against us. My father always told the story just in the same way as he would have related it at a grown-up dinner party, which was why we loved to hear him tell it to us. His own job in the *Agincourt* was to command No. 4 gun turret.

"On Wednesday 30th May 1915, the Grand Fleet left Scapa Flow in the Orkneys at 9.00 pm. There were 24 battleships with the 3rd battle cruiser squadrons, and the 4th light cruiser squadron, as well as the 4th, 11th and 12th destroyer flotillas, so it was a large fleet that sailed from Scapa Flow.

At 2.30 pm on the 31st, the *Agincourt* got a signal to raise steam for full speed, to at least 22 knots. (Her fuel was coal – man-handled by the whole ship's company, officers and men alike, when refuelling, which was a back-breaking and filthy job.)

At 3.00 pm they were told to "assume complete readiness for action in every respect" – a German cruiser had been sighted by H.M.S. *Galatea.*"

The rest of the story of the Battle of Jutland is well recorded in the history books. But my father's personal account continued to fascinate us. His ship was lucky to survive, in spite of being endangered by three torpedoes and straddled more than once by enemy salvoes. The only damage to the *Agincourt* came from one shell which burst short, and splintered part of the after-superstructure. It was here that my father, and his friend, Lieutenant Egerton, kept five white ferrets. "One of the splinters had split open their hutch and the ferrets were delighted to be given their liberty, so that they could explore the ship, until we recaptured them a week or two later, coal black from a bunker!" laughed my father.

We had heard this wonderful story many times before, but used to demand it again and again. My father never left out any of the technical bits, and, we responded to being given a serious description of the Battle of Jutland, complete with my father's own summing up of what went wrong, and why the battle had not turned out to be the glorious victory everyone had hoped for.

"Of course", he always ended, "one of the problems was that we never had enough destroyers. Nelson had the same problem at Trafalgar, a shortage of small frigates, and the signalling was atrocious! That's really why I decided to specialise in signals for the rest of my Naval career" he concluded.

It was now nearly time to get up, but we demanded a favourite game first. We sat in a row in bed, while one of us declaimed a list of birds and animals, and as soon as any bird was mentioned, the others had to flap their arms about in the air shouting "eagles fly", or "swallows fly". If, by mistake, we "flew" when an animal, and not a bird had been named, we were "out" (hence the name "Pigs Fly"). Like all simple games, it was one of the best and it always ended in great hilarity.

The astonishment of the young housemaid who arrived at this moment with the hot water cans, seeing us sitting in a bed covered with Christmas paper and ribbon, shrieking with mirth and waving our arms in the air, must have been complete. I wondered afterwards if Annie, who lived with her parents in Burnham, ever did things like that at home. I hoped she had some fun, and felt sorry for her having to do the chores for us at Hitcham on Christmas Day. We all wished her a very merry Christmas, and she told us that she was looking forward to the Christmas dinner Grannie had arranged for the staff in the Servants' Hall.

After breakfast, each member of the household had their own pile of exciting parcels laid out on a chair, and we set to, opening them with much dashing to and fro, to hug and kiss each other as we thanked for each present which was always "just what I wanted!". My mother and father gave me a beautiful china doll with eyes that opened and shut – she had long eyelashes and brown curly hair and I thought her quite lovely. I promptly christened her "Barbara", but I do not think I was aware that this was the name of my Cunninghame Graham grandmother, who was ending her days in a nursing home at Stoke Poges, and was sadly suffering from what we might now call Altzheimer's disease.

Then it was time for church, a little Norman church just across the road, to which we walked. The church was full of holly with scarlet berries and fir branches and yellow winter jasmine with hundreds of candles gleaming and flickering. Grannie and Grandfather sat in the front pew on the right, because Grandfather always read the lesson at the lectern, which was a gleaming brass eagle. The rest of us filled the pews immediately behind them. I liked to snuggle up beside my mother who wore the current fashion of silver fox furs. All the favourite hymns were sung, "Hark the Herald Angels", "Good Christian Men Rejoice", "The First Nowell", "While Shepherds Watched their Flocks by Night", and the final "Come all ye Faithful" with our local lady organist pulling out all the stops, and everyone singing heartily, the children loudest of all because they knew it meant that lunch would be next on the agenda.

Christmas lunch was another ritual (no different, probably, to almost every household in Britain). There was the huge turkey to be carved, with chestnut stuffing at one end, and sausage meat and herbs at the other; shining little chipolata sausages and golden roast potatoes; brussel sprouts and bread sauce. A meal fit for a king.

At Hitcham, it was the custom for the grandchildren to form a procession behind Massey when he brought in the Christmas pudding. After the first course we were allowed to join him in the butler's pantry, to watch him heating a little pan of brandy, setting it alight with a gorgeous burst of flame, and pouring it over the pudding, then we all trooped in behind the flaming pudding, to the grown-ups' satisfying oohs and aahs. Brandy butter was handed round and we always found small silver charms, and occasionally, a silver sixpence in our slice of pudding, which added to the excitement.

At the end of Christmas lunch everyone pulled their crackers and put on their paper hats, while I stood by miserably with my fingers in my ears. Once the bangs were over, I soon regained my high spirits as we all read out the silly cracker jokes and laughed uproariously, even if we were too young to understand the rather more doubtful jokes.

The Christmas tree was the real highlight of the day, later in the afternoon, and we shared it with everyone who worked for my grandparents. They came with all their families from the farm, and from all the cottages on the estate. These were the men my grandfather had formed into a battalion during the First World War, volunteers who were to become brave soldiers. Many of the families had lost a deeply loved husband, father and son in those dark days, which had only ended fifteen years ago.

The tree stood in the Garden Room, which was a large conservatory full of plants, and it was so tall that it almost touched the roof. We had helped Grannie to decorate it on Christmas Eve – there were little twisty candles clipped onto the branches with small decorative metal holders. In addition, there were sweets and oranges for all the children on the estate, which, we, the grandchildren, handed round, while grandfather and some helpers lit the candles till the whole tree seemed ablaze. I was relieved to see Bertram standing near with a sponge on a stick, in case of a holocaust.

Describing the ceremony today, it sounds feudal and patronising, but nobody thought of it like that, in those days. It was the highlight of the year for all the estate children and their parents, who knew it was my grandparents' way of saying thank you to them for all their loyalty and hard work. After tea, my mother played the piano, for musical bumps. This was followed by musical chairs, and the grown-ups all joined in. There was much laughter and enjoyment for all and we were a huge, happy family that Christmas Day. It was one of those rare occasions when social barriers crumble and we could laugh and make merry together, because we were all, in our different ways, linked to the microcosm that was Hitcham, which lay at the centre of our lives.

1934 arrived, and later in January a new cousin was born while we were still at Hitcham. My youngest uncle had married an enchanting red-haired wife, Lettice, early in 1933, and on 24th January, she gave birth to their son, Benjamin. We had seen a good deal of the young couple both at Hitcham, and at Lendrick. They had a house only a few miles away from Hitcham in the beautiful beech woods known as Burnham Beeches.

That night, I was out in the garden with my grandmother in the frosty moonlight. We looked up at the millions of stars twinkling in the clear night air, and she said "Quickly! Look! A shooting star! Perhaps a dear little baby will arrive tonight!" She must have known that my new aunt was already in labour, for sure enough, next morning, we heard the news that Christopher and Lettice had a son. I remember being particularly pleased that I would no longer be the youngest grandchild. It would be lovely to have a little boy to play with.

# CHAPTER VI

———◆◆◆———

MY FATHER JOINED the R.A.F. Staff College at Andover in the New Year and we moved to Hampshire. We found a small house in a village called Chilbolton. It was the first time we had lived in a village, and the little house had a cosy, protected feel. Now that I was nearly six, I was allowed to take the letters to the post box, and to fetch my comic, *Tiger Tim,* from the little shop on the corner. This was my first taste of real independence, and I thoroughly enjoyed it.

By now, I was not missing Nanny quite so much – perhaps because she wrote to me regularly and affectionately, so I knew she still loved me and I now knew, too, that it was nothing that I had done which had caused her to leave. Also, I got to know our Swiss nursery governess, Elsa, much better now, and found that she was rather fun to be with. She enjoyed getting Robin and me to act little plays for our parents, and she was always full of ideas of interesting things to do.

At this point, I started school. I remember nothing about it, except that there was a girl of my age called Janet who wore spectacles, and that we had to answer the morning roll-call with the Latin word "Adsum". None of us six-year-olds had the faintest idea what it meant.

The school was in Andover so my father took me there, on his way to work, in our little Morris car, which had a "dickey" at the back. The days of the Bean and the Bentley were over, now that my father's meagre Naval pay was being stretched in so many new ways, including the fees for my brother's expensive prep school, Pinewood, at Farnborough. I loved those journeys with my father, because we used to make up songs, which we sang as we rolled along.

The new speed limit, in built-up areas, had just been introduced, and we sang a song of my father's which went:

> "Thirty we must go, thirty seems so slow!
>   We mustn't go at forty, for that is very naughty,
>   We mustn't go at fifty, it really isn't thrifty.
>   And sixty, seventy, eighty makes the policeman very
>     batey!"

Later in the year, when haymaking was in full progress, my father made up another song, most of the words of which I have forgotten but which conjured up this typical countryside scene so well:

> "They're making the hay in the meadow!
>   They're making the hay in the meadow
>   And old Farmer Wapstraw is drinking his ale.
>   As they're making the hay in the meadow!"

. . . and so on. It had a wonderful tune, which I have never forgotten and I now realise that making up tunes, as well as funny words, was another of my father's many talents.

We always passed the same people, and children, going to work or to school on our morning run, and used to refer to them by names we made up. On one occasion, after dropping me at my school, my father was astonished to see one of his wheels bowling off ahead of him down the road. The car swerved suddenly and came to a halt in a lopsided fashion, as my father hastily put on the brake. These were the sort of things that happened in those early days of motoring. Fortunately, there was still very little other traffic about, and neither he nor the car were any the worse.

I remember one other thing about my first school which demonstrates that I was either extremely stupid, or that the teaching was not of the highest standard – probably a bit of both. I used to be presented with attractive cards on which were drawn coloured pictures of dolls, rubber balls, toy sailing ships and ice-cream cones, to each of these objects was attached a label, and on this label I was supposed to write down how much the object cost. I had not the faintest idea, and was never quite clear why I should be expected to know. Naturally, I wrote down anything that came into my head, and my school mistress was very cross with me. I never did discover the point of those cards.

To make up for my stupidity at sums, I found I was one of the best readers and spellers in the class, which redeemed me somewhat in the eyes of the worthy ladies who ran the little school. "Sums" were never to be my great strength, until I was forced into the practical mathematics of house-keeping; and later, fund-raising, after which I suddenly found that everything I had been taught made sense after all.

After school, I used to go for walks with Elsa. We lived on the edge of the Downs, and they were the happiest and most rewarding walks I ever remember. I have a vivid memory of picking a tiny bunch of the sweetest smelling white violets in a hedge, and presenting them to my father on his birthday which was on 16th February. We must have had a very early spring that year. I also remember the new green leaves beginning to appear in the hedges, which I used to pick and eat. Obviously, I ate the most extraordinary things in those days: new green leaves, dog biscuits, and once at Hitcham I took a bite out of a quince, thinking it was a large yellow pear. That was one of my least successful experiments as a budding gourmet. A quince tastes incredibly bitter, and I can never understand why quince jelly is so sweet and delectable.

I was having fewer bad colds by the spring of 1934, and life was a great deal happier than it had been during the previous winter at Hitcham. But, in spite of that, I still knew that Hitcham was my favourite place to be. We had now acquired a new dog – not a small puppy this time, my parents not wishing to risk another tragedy – but a brisk, six-month-old wire-haired terrier. We called him Rogie (II). Rogie, like all terriers, was energetic, aggressive and inquisitive. He loved fighting, and I dreaded most of all meeting another dog on our walks, because Rogie always started the fight, and usually won it. It was extremely embarrassing, and I used to disown him; but nevertheless, I was very fond of him, as I was, and still am, of all dogs.

Three months after settling into our cosy village-house in Chilbolton, the Naval couple from whom we had rented it were suddenly brought home, unexpectedly, from an overseas post. They naturally wanted their house back. Fortunately, we were able to move into another house not far away and in the same village. It was called "Down End", and its name described it perfectly – it stood on the edge of the Downs, on a hill just outside the village. Compared with our first house, I thought it very large and grand, but on revisiting it many years later as a nostalgic adult, I found to my surprise that it was not nearly as big as I had originally thought. I remember thinking that it was the most perfect house we had ever lived in.

There was wisteria under my bedroom window, which was just coming out. This was the pale mauve of my favourite colour, the mauve of fairy's wings, and of my *Cardiff* birthday cake, once more. There was also a huge lawn, and a pretty garden surrounded by pale green beech trees. My particular memory of Down End is of waking very early in the morning before five, and tiptoeing downstairs in my bare feet to run on the lawn, as the birds were beginning to sing their dawn chorus. I was truly in fairy-land, with dew on the grass and the beech leaves rustling as a tiny breath of air passed between the branches. The sun crept round the east end of the house like a torch shining round a corner. Bees were already buzzing in the wisteria, but no-one else was awake. I had the whole garden to myself, perhaps even the whole world. This is still one of my happiest memories of my whole childhood.

Elsa was really supposed to talk French with us, but as she came from Zurich, in the German speaking part of Switzerland, her French wasn't very good. She was not allowed to teach us German, because my parents were still very prejudiced against Germans since the horrors of the First World War.

I remember she told me in her very bad French, that a grapefruit was a "pumple-mouse" which I thought was a delicious word. (My father's favourite French word was "topinambour", which means a Jerusalem artichoke.)

For my sixth birthday I was given a white rabbit with pink eyes (the sort the French breed to eat), and I called him, with a total lack of originality, "Peter".

I don't think he had a very nice nature, and when I went to stroke him, he used to make a strange growling sound which was far from friendly. Nevertheless, I liked picking dandelion leaves for him, and cleaning out his hutch while he lolloped round his run.

I still played a great deal with my family of dolls, and I now read every children's book I could lay my hands on. I read so much that my mother gave me a subscription to Harrods' Children's Library, and I can still remember the magic of the open-ended parcels, which used to arrive weekly to keep up with my literary appetite.

I always read lying on my tummy, which meant that my eyes were much too near the page, and I can still hear my mother saying, "How can you read like that, darling? It's *so* bad for your eyes!". The authors I liked best were E. Nesbit, Arthur Ransome, and Harrison Ainsworth, whose historical books often seemed to relate to my imaginary Elizabethan family.

At night I used to smuggle a torch under my pillow so that I could read under the bedclothes when I was meant to be asleep. Eventually, when I had gone through not only two books, but also a new torch battery, in a couple of nights, Elsa "twigged", and the torch was confiscated.

When Robin came home for the summer holidays, my mother gave a children's party, as it was half-way between my May birthday and my brother's September one. I only remember this because we have a friend (who is now, like me, middle-aged) who came to that party as a small boy. His father was in the Navy too, and owned some dry-fly fishing on the Test which my father used to enjoy. We ended the party with a game my mother had invented – a "treasure hunt" round the garden, looking for haricot beans (the hard, dry white sort) which she had hidden. The child who found the largest number of beans won the prize. Poor Gerard Buxton did not know what a "haricot bean" was, so he had no idea what he was meant to be looking for, and ended the game with no beans at all. We met again when we were both grown-up, and he told me the sad story. His elder sister overheard me sympathising with him, and said rather harshly, "Rubbish, he was just a *wet* little boy!" I thought she was very unfair. I could hardly bear to think of the misery it must have caused him, all those years ago.

In 1935, my father was appointed Staff Officer Operations to Admiral Sir Hugh Tweedie, the Commander-in-Chief of the Nore, at Chatham. This job was a great deal better than attending Staff Colleges, which had been rather like being back at school. Admiral Tweedie had been his C-in-C in Simonstown so he already knew him well. My father had now been a Commander for seven years, and only had one more year to go, before being "passed over" for promotion. The rather tough system was that all the Commanders in the Navy were put into batches, and each batch had only a fixed quota of promotions given to them in an eight year promotion zone.

It was a great worry for serving officers to think that they might be retired by the age of 40, when to change your way of life becomes much more difficult, just as it is probably much harder for an older man to get a job outside the Navy. Worst of all, they were unlikely to go to sea again, which is what they had joined the Navy for in the first place.

My father was particularly nervous because he knew that no Commander who had held a staff appointment to the C-in-C of a home port, had ever been promoted. In the end of the day, he need not have worried but he was not to know that until 31st December 1935.

Meanwhile, being a man who never "crossed his bridges before he got to them", he decided to enjoy his job just as he had enjoyed all the others. This meant another move for us, and we were offered a fine Elizabethan half-timbered house in the village of Hartlip in Kent. This village now features on a signpost on the M20, being only two miles to the east of the big motorway, on the way to Dover. The house was on a hilltop and as we moved there in mid-winter, it was extremely cold. But I loved it because it was of the same period as my imaginary Elizabethan family, who still played a continuous part in my rather solitary life.

It is strange the tricks memories can play, and how time gets distorted in childhood, and I was sure we had lived at Down End in Chilbolton for years and years before we moved to Hartlip. In fact, we can only have lived there for less than nine months. We moved to Queendown Warren just after Christmas, at the beginning of 1935.

Once again, the owner unexpectedly wanted his house back only a few months after we had moved in, so we had to move yet again, this time to a house in the next village of Newington near Sittingbourne. It was a small house beside a cherry orchard and, having got well used to being perpetually on the move, we had soon settled in very happily. This was our fourth move within fifteen months. Strangely enough, I have no recollection of the constant packing and unpacking that must have accompanied our moves, which shows what a good home-maker my mother was, and how smoothly she arranged our lives.

Elsa left us just after we moved to the Newington house. I suspect my parents found the expense of a nursery governess too great. In her place came what we would now call a French "au-pair" girl, and I was perfectly horrid to her. She was not very attractive to look at, a thin and bony young woman with a drip permanently at the end of her nose. Presumably, like the majority of au-pair girls, she had been sent by her parents to learn English and was not particularly interested in looking after children. I can't believe that she stayed very long with us, and only remember that I disliked her intensely. I probably drove her away with my unpleasant behaviour, poor Yvonne.

I now went to school at Chatham. It was a small class run by the Royal Engineers, or "The Sappers", in their barracks. I had a real friend for the first time in my life, she was called Elizabeth. Elizabeth's father was a Sapper Colonel. Both the Royal Engineers' Barracks, and the Naval Barracks, were at Chatham. Elizabeth was an only child, so her parents liked to have me to stay for the night from time to time to keep her company. As Robin was away at school, the arrangement was of mutual benefit. We soon found that we were kindred spirits, and our friendship grew.

It was very good for me to have a friend of my own age for the first time. I was not a naturally introverted child, but I had spent far too much time on my own, relying on my own imagination for entertainment. Elizabeth and I enjoyed ourselves doing all the things that six and seven-year-olds like doing together. We drew and painted, we played shops and houses, we had dolls' tea-parties and we occasionally did the things we had been specifically told not to do. I am sure, as a result, I became a nicer child, and not quite so taken up with myself. Elizabeth and I also went to a dancing class and wore real "tu-tu's" made by our mothers for our end-of-term display.

For my seventh birthday, my mother invited the children who attended my small school to a party at Chesley, as well as two brothers we had met when we lived at Hartlip. They were called Robin and Nigel. This friendship led on to one of the most enjoyable activities of my whole childhood. The Leigh Pembertons used to organise a football game from time to time in a field in front of their house and invite all their friends' children to play, both boys and girls. When he grew up, Robin was to have a brilliant career as a banker, and I now enjoy telling my friends how I used to play football with the Governor of the Bank of England.

That summer was the Silver Jubilee of King George V and Queen Mary, who had been on the throne for twenty-five years. My father's elder sister was married to a naval officer who had left the Navy and become Controller of the Duke of York's household; this was the younger Royal brother who was soon to become King George VI. My mother and Robin were invited to watch the Silver Jubilee procession from a special stand for the royal household in the forecourt of Buckingham Palace, but my father had to be on duty at Chatham, and I was, presumably, considered too young to go with them.

To make up for my disappointment, my father took me, a few days later, to a reception given for Queen Marie of Romania at the C-in-C's house in Chatham. All the European kings and queens had come to London for the celebrations, and I suppose they were being entertained in various ways for the rest of their visit.

I was told that Queen Marie had been one of the most beautiful of all the queens, and that I was very lucky to be allowed to go with my father. I think she had known him as a small boy, when my grandfather (who had died during the First World War) had also been in the royal household.

My father told me I would be presented to Queen Marie and that I must curtsey to her. I had learnt to curtsey at my dancing class, so I was not at all worried about that. I remember the party vividly – it was quite a small gathering, and I think I was probably the only child there. I felt very grown-up and important, but, looking round me, I could see no-one who looked in the least like a queen. While I was staring round, an old lady in black, and wearing pearls came up to talk to my father and to me. She asked me about my school and was very friendly. Then she moved off to talk to someone else. My father looked at me very crossly and said "Why didn't you curtsey?". I was covered with confusion – how was I supposed to know that the nice old lady in black was Queen Marie? She hadn't even got a crown on.

That summer the cherries seemed to grow larger and more luscious than anyone had ever seen them. Elizabeth would come to Chesley to stay the night, and we gorged ourselves on Napoleons and White Hearts from the orchard beside our garden. I suspect our neighbours must have told my mother that we could help ourselves for I do not remember getting into trouble for it. In those days, Kent seemed to be one huge orchard, and where the fruit trees stopped, the hops began. Londoners from the east end would come to do the picking – huge cheerful groups of Cockneys who brought their children and made a holiday of it.

Two things happened that winter: one nice and the other nasty. The first was our school nativity play, in which I was a donkey. I remember my tail was made out of a brown woolly dressing-gown cord with a large tassel on the end. I enjoyed my part enormously, and was not at all envious of Elizabeth who had been chosen to be Mary, and who looked beautiful with a pale blue shawl covering her fair hair. All the parents came and we felt it was the most important thing we had ever done in our lives, especially when the clapping and cheering went on for ages as we stood in a row on the stage looking extremely pleased with ourselves.

The nasty thing happened after Christmas.

# CHAPTER VII

T HE "NASTY" THING started off by being something I had been looking forward to for days. Robin had arrived home for the Christmas holidays and we had both been invited to the Royal Marine's annual children's party in Chatham Barracks. Everyone told me that it was the best children's party of the year. I remembered parties on board H.M.S. *Cardiff* and already knew that parties run by sailors (or in this case, the Marines) were always far more fun than parties run by mothers. I was also told that the famous Royal Marine Band would play at it, whom I had already heard playing when we went with my father to church in Chatham Barracks on Sundays.

It was to be a Fancy Dress Party. My brother wore the court page's costume that my father had worn at the age of nine at King Edward VII's Coronation, and I wore a Dutch boy's outfit, that had been my brother's: baggy blue trousers that fitted on to huge buttons on my orange jacket and tall hat.

The party had only just begun when the accident happened. The first thing we saw when we arrived was a huge children's slide which had been erected in the big drill hall in which the party took place. It was no ordinary slide, but more like one at a fun-fair – you climbed a tall ladder, and then swooped up and down on a switchback for what seemed like several minutes, before arriving safely on the thick coconut matting at the bottom where two of the Marines stood on either side to catch you and to help you up.

Everyone wanted to go on that slide. I had already had *one* "go", and was queueing up for my next turn. The Marine Band, placed under the huge arch of the slide, were playing jolly tunes as the queue of children in fancy dress moved slowly forward and up the ladder to the top. Being wise after the event, I suppose one of the organisers should have realised that the structure, strong as it was, could not bear the weight of so many children on the ladder at the same time.

Suddenly, with a loud cracking sound, the whole structure collapsed, flinging children in all directions, with heavy pieces of the slide crashing down on the heads of the unfortunate bandsmen underneath. Most of the children were flung clear, and merely bruised and frightened. I was the unlucky one: my leg had got caught in one of the rungs of the ladder and I broke my ankle in several places (a "Pott's fracture", they told us later at the hospital in Rochester). One of the bandsmen was severely injured, too, and we landed up in hospital together.

I can remember my thoughts quite clearly as the slide began to collapse. I had great faith in grown-ups, as all children have whose childhood is secure and happy. Surely, if they were arranging this party for our enjoyment, this must be *meant* to be happening? Grown-ups loved giving children nice surprises, perhaps we were all descending to a cave below where there would be pirates handing out chocolate money? (I well remembered the pirates at our parties on board the *Cardiff.*) But when I landed on the ground, still tangled in the broken rungs of the ladder, I decided that this treat really hadn't been much fun. I had an excruciating pain in my leg, and when I tried to get up I couldn't walk. I also felt rather sick.

To his great credit, my brother got to my side before anyone else. "I can't walk!" I whimpered. Then I was surrounded by grown-ups and carried through to the Commanding Officer's house, which was next to the Drill Hall. I was still dressed as a Dutch boy.

The account in the local paper said "After the accident, the children were taken to tea". Robin had not wanted to leave me, but Mrs Craig, the Commanding Officer's wife, was now in full control and had already telephoned my mother. So Robin was persuaded to join the other children and taken off, somewhat reluctantly, while I lay on a sofa, wrapped in rugs with Mrs Craig holding my hand and showing me her cage of budgerigars. I remember being in very great pain at the time, but I think I was perfectly controlled. After all, I was a sailor's daughter, and Nanny used to tell me that sailors' daughters never cried. Perhaps she had told me once too often, for I was seldom, for the rest of my life, able to relieve grief or frustration with tears, as other people can do.

I suppose I was gratified to be told after the event that I had been "very brave", but I was really just a very damaged small child, longing for her mother to come.

I believe my mother had not been at home when she was first telephoned and it seemed a long time till she came. However, shortly after she arrived, I went with her to Rochester Hospital – and for the next two weeks I went through many frightening and miserable experiences. My leg was immediately set, after I had been given a terrifying anaesthetic which was a muslin bag soaked in chloroform, held over my nose so that I not only felt that I was being suffocated but I could also hear a loud booming noise until I slipped into blessed unconsciousness.

But it was not deep unconsciousness even then, because I had terrifying nightmares throughout, until I came round once more to be violently sick. It was the most inhumane process, so different to the painless injections given nowadays, and the peaceful feeling of "disappearing", before you can even count to ten. Even worse, they did not set it right first time round and a few days later I had to go through the whole horrifying process once again.

The shock to my system must have been intense for I went on having nightmares almost every night for more than a year after I came out of hospital.

While I was in hospital, two important things had taken place: the first was that my father had been promoted to Captain, to his total astonishment and relief, on 31st December 1935. This meant that his career was assured, and he was ultimately to serve in the Royal Navy for a total of 46 years.

"It was a miraculous moment in my life," he was to say later.

A few weeks later, King George V died, to be greatly mourned by the whole nation. A great many people wore black or purple in those days when the King died, and the serving officers all wore black armbands.

# CHAPTER VIII

───────◆◆◆───────

ALL THE KINGS AND queens arrived once more for the sad occasion of the King Emperor's funeral, and as the royal household could not possibly look after them all, Captains, Colonels, and Group Captains were brought to London to help. My father was asked to help Sir Philip Hunloke to look after Prince Paul of Greece, who had come to represent his brother, the King of Greece.

The Greek royal family were, surprisingly, really of *Danish* extraction. My father told us that Prince Paul referred to his brother's subjects, most affectionately, as "those bloody Greeks". In fact, both the King of Greece and Prince Paul (who was later to succeed his brother as King) had dedicated their lives to Greece, and were extremely proud of their Greek subjects and of the whole Greek ethos.

Queen Victoria's grand-daughter had married into the Greek royal family, so they were all close cousins of King George V, whose funeral the large family of the old Queen were all anxious to attend. Princess Alice, the daughter of Prince Louis of Battenberg, had also married into the Greek royal family and was to bear four girls, followed, a long ime later, by a boy, Philip of Greece, who was later to become Duke of Edinburgh and husband of our Queen. This meant that Prince Louis of Battenberg was the Duke of Edinburgh's grandfather.

Prince Louis of Battenberg had been my grandfather's shipmate in the Royal Navy, and his greatest friend. In fact, they looked so alike that they were often mistaken for each other.

Charles Cunninghame Graham and the young German prince both attended the same "crammer" in Gosport before sitting their entrance examination for the Royal Navy. They both passed and became cadets, being exactly the same age. In due course they both went to sea as midshipmen, joining the same ship, H.M.S. *Ariadne*. Prince Louis was given an extremely rough time by the gunroom, and it was my grandfather, his friend and fellow "snotty", who defended the German prince from the xenophobic young Naval officers, who could not understand why he wanted to join the British Navy. Prince Louis was to suffer all his life from a prejudice against his German extraction, even though his wife was Queen Victoria's grand-daughter. But he never forgot his friend Charlie Cunninghame Graham's friendship and loyalty, and it was Prince Louis who recommended my grandfather for a fascinating new appointment, after he had been invalided out of the Navy as a commander, to be Deputy Chief Inspector of Lifeboats – a whole new career connected with the sea, which was his passion. Later still, Prince Louis recommended my grandfather as a Groom-in-Waiting to King Edward VII, and subsequently to King George V.

The children of members of the royal household have traditionally been given ceremonial duties on special occasions, and my father's summons to look after Prince Paul while he attended King George V's funeral was probably one of these sorts of occasions. As a small boy he had been a page-of-honour to the Duke of Fife at King Edward VII's coronation, mainly because he was the King's godson. I now have a son-in-law who has also been a page-of-honour, to the Queen, at a special service in St. George's Chapel at Windsor, for exactly the same reason – his father, Sir Rennie Maudslay, was a member of the royal household as Keeper of the Privy Purse. So history continues to repeat itself, most fascinatingly.

Although my grandfather knew Prince Louis so well, my father's own naval career did not bring him nearly so closely in touch with Prince Louis' son Lord Louis Mountbatten, known as "Dickie". Lord Mountbatten was seven years younger than my father, which was another reason. However, they had lived next door to each other in Malta, the year before I was born, in 1927. When I was nineteen I went to a concert at the Edinburgh Festival with Lady Mountbatten, because her own daughter, Pamela, had been unable to go with her at the last minute. (The Mountbattens were staying with my parents at Rosyth, where my father was C-in-C Scotland and Northern Ireland.) I found the experience distinctly daunting, although it was kind of her to take me. She seemed to know everyone at the concert including the conductor, Sir Malcolm Sargent, and I felt very shy and gauche. Many years later my mother, in her late eighties, was chatting to our local doctor about her young days. "We had rather noisy neighbours when we lived in Malta," she told him. He was much amused when he later discovered she had been referring to Lord and Lady Mountbatten.

While my father was attached to Prince Paul for the royal funeral, he experienced a very touching event. The night before the funeral they all dined at Buckingham Palace. And because my father's brother-in-law, Basil Brooke, was also in the royal household, he was let into the secret that the four royal brothers, the Duke of York, the Duke of Kent, Prince Henry, Duke of Gloucester, and their brother, the new King Edward VIII, were going to leave the party early and take up position at the four corners of their father's coffin on the catafalque in Westminster Hall. My father was able to extract Prince Paul from the party and drove him to Westminster Hall, where they saw the four royal brothers standing round their father's coffin with their hands on the hilts of their reversed swords and their heads bowed. It was a moving sight.

During my father's year at Chatham, he and his admiral, Admiral Sir Hugh Tweedie, had plenty to keep them occupied. They were already preparing for the war that was to be declared only four years later and were particularly involved with air raid precautions. Their first job was to discover how best to "black-out" the three towns, Chatham, Gillingham and Rochester. Because of the dockyard machinery, local industry and hospitals, it would be impractical to switch off the power, so they had to start to train industry, large establishments and individuals to black-out their own lights. But a trial black-out was not allowed by the government who refused it because they were worried that it would cause panic. My father's own view was that the brave and phlegmatic people of Kent (as these people so valiantly proved to be, during the war) would take such a precaution in their stride.

My father also proposed a dummy dockyard on the mudflats of the Medway, to attract enemy bombs away from the real yard. This idea was much used during the Second World War. Ironically, one of several dummy "towns" on the Clyde, away from the shipyards, was situated barely a mile from our own home. I suspect it was an unqualified success for, one night, 400 high explosive bombs were dropped by the Germans within a radius of three miles of our own village – the nearest shipyard, Denny's in Dumbarton, being well out of their range. Fortunately we survived our private "blitz", as I shall tell in a subsequent chapter, with only a relatively small amount of damage to our house, though the village suffered a great deal worse.

But in 1935, as a child of seven, I was quite unaware that precautions for the possibility of another war were already under way, and my own life was peaceful and happy in the extreme, once I had got over my traumatic experience in hospital.

I had another treat after I came out of hospital. I was taken to watch the launching of a new submarine, H.M.S. *Grampus*. A new C-in-C had recently succeeded Admiral Tweedie. He was Admiral Teddy Evans, who had accompanied Scott on his expedition to the Antarctic, and also the man who had succeeded Admiral Tweedie in the same job in Simonstown. We knew him well. The two admirals seemed to be playing a private game of "follow-my-leader" in their Naval careers. His wife, Elsa, was Norwegian and I remember her launching the submarine with the words, "I name this ship 'Grrampooos'". I thought it was a wonderful name for a ship.

In March 1936 my father's uncle, the distinguished writer and traveller, Robert Bontine Cunninghame Graham (known to many as "Don Roberto"), died on a nostalgic visit to Buenos Aires, where he had spent part of his youth. He was in his 84th year. As he was childless (his rather theatrical wife, "Gabrielle", whose real name was Caroline Horsfall, had died in 1906), my father was his heir. This meant that we suddenly became very much better off than we had ever been before, and it also meant that we had suddenly become the owners of no less than three houses: one in Dunbartonshire, on the River Clyde; one at Rothesay on the Island of Bute; and one in London. An "embarras de richesse!"

Ardoch, the little family house built near Dumbarton Rock in 1790 by our forbear Robert Graham of Gartmore, was to be our first real home, and my father and mother were overjoyed at the thought of having a home of their own at last.

The house in London turned out to be useful for a year or two, but as we could not afford to keep up two houses, so this, too, was sold before long. It was in Elizabeth Street, just across from Chester Square. My great-uncle had bought the house after the First World War to be near his mother, my great-grandmother, who lived to the great age of 97, in her own house in Chester Square. She died in 1925, the year my brother was born; so I never knew her, but I have often thought she and I had much in common, both of us inheriting a strong streak of Spanish blood, which made our lives more exciting, and more argumentative, into the bargain. All Spaniards thrive on argument, which they think of as an intellectual game and a useful way of learning about other people's opinions.

With the Elizabeth Street house, we acquired Mrs Heathcote. She had been my great-uncle's housekeeper for many years and came straight out of a Dickens novel. She was small and bony and very old, and whenever she went out, she put on a black bonnet with purple ribbon tied under her chin. She wore a long black dress (probably made of bombazine, I suspect), and indoors she always wore an apron. She was usually rather lugubrious, but she ran the house perfectly and I think she must have done all the cooking as well, as I do not remember there being any other servants there.

I was to feel that we must have lived for several years at our house, Chesley, in Kent, just as I had felt about Down End in Hampshire. In fact we only lived for less than a year in each of these two houses. Strange unconnected memories come to me in flashes from those years, like a series of slides on a projector. One is particularly vivid:

My Aunt "Woggie", my mother's elder sister Rachel, had come to stay. She was a beautiful woman with a warm personality and I was always to feel that I could talk to her about anything under the sun and she would understand. When my first marriage was to break up thirty years later, she was the first person in whom I felt I could confide. I always felt, as a child, probably quite wrongly, that my mother was far too busy to listen to my doubts and fancies. Aunt Woggie seemed to have all the time in the world, even in her own house, to relax in a chair and talk. She and my mother were the Martha and the Mary of their family.

The incident that is so clearly stamped in my mind must have been around Guy Fawkes Day, because I had been to a fireworks party in a house in Kent that was within walking distance of Chesley. (Not my favourite sort of party, because I hated the bangs, although I loved the bonfire itself.) My aunt came to fetch me from the party and we walked home together over the hill by a country lane on a still clear night with the whole black velvet arch of the sky spangled with more stars than I could believe possible.

"That's the Milky Way," said my aunt pointing, "and that's Orion. Oh, and look! That very bright one, low down, that's Venus." (My father had told us about the stars too, for sailors still used them to steer by, in spite of all their newly developing technology.) Then we walked on in silence, and I could hear the sharp high bark of a vixen, and an owl hooting in a nearby tree.

"Isn't it lovely!" I said, and my aunt agreed. Then I remember a tickle developed on the sole of my foot, so I started stamping my left foot with each step to try to get rid of the tickle. My aunt burst out laughing. "What a funny way to walk!" she said, as my feet went "Step, stump, step, stump" along the road.

"I've got a tickle in my foot," I explained, and we both giggled all the way home. That was all there was to the incident, but it was a happy one and those small, happy incidents of childhood are like pearls in a jewel-box, always lying there to be cherished and treasured, taken out and remembered as small flashes of beauty.

We still went to stay at my beloved Hitcham from time to time and I loved to visit my uncle and aunt in Burnham Beeches and play with my new cousin, Ben, who was now an attractive two-year-old. My chronology is vague at this time, but I think it was during the summer, of 1935, that we were at Hitcham for the Fourth of June celebrations at Eton College. Every year, my grandmother gave a huge lunch-party at Hitcham on the Fourth of June for the Eton boys she knew, and their parents. Her own two sons had been at Eton, and the college lay only a few miles from Hitcham on its site near the water meadows of the Thames, under the shadow of Windsor Castle.

To get there, we used to go across Dorney Common, which to this day, still remains the epitome of the "common-land" of mediaeval times. Because it was common grazing (in other words "free for all"), there were donkeys, circus ponies, and other unusual animals wandering about on the common, some of them hobbled. We drove across Dorney Common with my grandmother in her large square Armstrong Siddeley, driven by Berry, the chauffeur, who wore spectacles and alarmed us all because we were never quite sure how much he could really see.

That Fourth of June in 1935 was to prove particularly memorable for me. First, there was the lunch party, at Hitcham, at which I sat next to a jolly seventeen-year-old called Donald Graham, who watched me enjoying Emily's superb meringues

(shaped like a large mushroom and filled with chocolate cream)
and told me I would burst.

"That's a good name for her 'Burstie'!" teased one of my
uncles. "Like the one in the church!" said another of my uncles.
I was mystified. The name was to stick for a long time, to my
acute embarrassment. It was only a year ago that I went back to
Hitcham and attended a service in St. Mary's Church, at the end
of the drive. Gazing round the memorials while waiting for the
service to begin I suddenly saw on one of them the name
"Burstie" – so *that* was why they knew it, all those years ago,
and thought it suited me.

That night my grandmother took me to the fireworks
display at Eton, and to watch the procession of boats. Little did
I realise at the time that a friend of Donald Graham's called
Harry Scott who was "Ninth Man of the Monarch", carefully
balancing in *The Monarch* with his oar aloft and the traditional
wreath of flowers round his boater, was eventually to be my
second husband. I don't suppose I picked him out that night,
but I thought the ten young oarsmen looked like Greek gods,
and fell madly in love with all of them, as seven-year-olds are
apt to do. It was a very special treat, and I was always to
remember the beautiful set pieces of the fireworks display,
including the ingenious little firework acrobat who did a
trapeze act, and the roars of delight of the watching crowds as
he successfully leapt from one sparkly rope to another. It was an
evening of utter enchantment.

In August, we went to Lendrick once more, to my great
delight. My grandparents had a great many guests that year, so
we children went to stay in a nearby farmhouse. I think Elsa
must have come back to look after us for the holidays, because
I know she was there with us. All my cousins were there as
well, and we were allowed to go camping by ourselves in a
pretty wood beside a burn not far from Lendrick. The boys shot
rabbits with their four-ten guns, and caught trout in the burn, so
we ate well, cooking them on our campfire. We all slept in a
bell-tent and were considerably frightened one night by an eery
whistling sound. It turned out to be the air escaping from

Robin's air cushion – anti-climax, and hysterical giggles all round!

In the autumn of 1936 my father received an exciting summons from the Naval Secretary in Whitehall to proceed to Hong Kong, forthwith, to be "Senior Naval Officer, West River, China".

It was the best job going for a junior captain, but my father must have had mixed feelings about his imminent departure to the Far East, having so recently inherited Ardoch and a house in London, and knowing that he would have to leave my mother behind to cope with everything at home. He hoped to have her brought out, with me, by P&O in due course, once everything was arranged, and once he had been able to find a house in Hong Kong. But Robin would have to stay at school in England, for he was inevitably heading for the Royal Navy, and had to take his entrance examination for Dartmouth within two years. It was a stiff exam and he had to work hard for his final two years at his "prep" school, if he was to succeed. Preparatory schools usually prepared boys for public schools – which, of course, are really private schools – but as boys who wished to become Naval Cadets (before the Second World War) went to The Royal Naval College at Dartmouth when they were thirteen, most of them attended prep schools first.

In those days, when the journey to Hong Kong by sea took six weeks, there were no flights for school children to join their parents for the holidays. But when my mother had married a Naval Officer she had her eyes wide open and she knew it would mean many partings and separations.

# CHAPTER IX

───────●──◆──●───────

URING THE EASTER holidays in 1936, before my
father left for China, we had our first and last holiday
abroad, in France and Spain, for my father's annual
leave. Although we had travelled more than most children, we
had never gone for a holiday together as a family. Since he had
been left some money by his uncle, it was the first time he could
afford to take us abroad for such a holiday. It was also the first
time I had been to the Continent, and I was fascinated. South
Africa had always seemed exceptionally "British", as indeed it
was in those days; living in the same way as we lived at home,
but under a different climate. Everyone talked English in South
Africa and we did not even hear much Afrikaans spoken
because our Afrikaans friends always, very politely, talked to
us in English, as did our coloured servants.

To cross the Channel and hear French spoken, to smell the
"Caporal" cigarettes, and to eat the garlicky food, was all
tremendously stimulating to me. It felt far more "abroad" than
anywhere else I had ever been.

The first night, we stayed at the Hotel Meurice in Paris,
before catching our train to St. Jean de Luz. As the train
departed late at night, I was allowed to stay up for dinner. It was
the first time I had ever had a meal in a hotel, and I thought it
very grand. What intrigued me most of all were the large
numbers of small children, wearing their "party clothes", who

were sitting up having dinner with their parents. I had not realised that this was a normal state of affairs in France. Francoise Monod, a very dear French friend, was to say to me recently, "You know, our children in France don't get nearly enough sleep. That is why we French are all so nervy!".

As always, my memories were fixed by subtle new tastes. I had my first praline ice for dinner that night, and I can still remember the delicious taste of toasted almonds. At the station I spotted boiled sweets wrapped in cellophane to look like luscious bunches of purple and green grapes, and persuaded my mother to buy them for me; and at the bookstall she bought me a cheap, but attractively illustrated edition of *Les Malheurs de Sophie,* which was to become one of my favourite books.

In the dedication by the author, the Comtesse de Segur (née Sophie Rostopchine) to Elisabeth Fresnau, she says to her little grand-daughter:

"Chère enfant, tu me dis souvent 'Oh grandmère, que je vous aime. Vous êtes si bonne!' Grandmère n'a pas toujours été bonne ... Voicie des histoires vrais d'une petite fille que grandmère a beaucoup connue dans son enfance ..."

The Comtesse de Segur was one of the first authors ever to write (as early as the 1850's) about naughty children. Naturally, her book immediately became every child's favourite, just as it was to become one of mine, once I had mastered the French in which it was written, with the help of my mother. The large illustrations in my own rather gaudy, cheap edition also helped enormously with my comprehension. They showed quite clearly all the mischief Sophie got up to, and I loved the book dearly. I now have a grand-daughter called Sophie, but I think she is probably too poetic and busy with her own fascinating thoughts to have time for conventional "naughtiness" like her French counterpart.

When we got to St. Jean de Luz, we stayed in a large hotel beside the beach, rather like a hotel in Torquay. I found it all rather dispiriting after tasting the delights of Paris. This was just an ordinary seaside town with a deserted beach covered with pebbles and a cold wind blowing in from the grey Atlantic. The fact that it was early April and still "out of season" probably explained my disappointment (I believe the beach nowadays has beautiful golden sand imported and spread along the edge of the sea). I think I was also suffering from "traveller's tummy", as I remember feeling rather sick most of the time we were in St. Jean de Luz.

There were plenty of amusements however, and I enjoyed making friends with a large family of very cosmopolitan children all of whom, down to a very pretty and precocious black-eyed three-year-old, seemed to speak about five different languages. I think they were probably originally Spanish, but had travelled all over the Continent with their parents, and I much enjoyed playing on the beach with them.

There was also an old man with an intelligent fox-terrier who showed us that he could pick up a pebble off the stony beach (on which he then made a mark with a piece of chalk), and when he threw it, the dog always brought him back the right one. We were amazed by the cleverness of this small dog.

I don't think we stayed very long at St. Jean de Luz, because our next stop was at Fontarabia, where we bought castanets. Robin and I hung out of the car windows clicking our castanets at pedestrians, until my father told us quite sharply to desist. Civil disturbance was already affecting the north of Spain and the Basque country, and both the French police and the Guarda Civil were distinctly jumpy. My father was convinced that they would decide that we were being provocative and clap us all in jail. A few months later the Spanish Civil War began in earnest.

In Fontarabia we watched the young men playing their national game of pelota – a sort of mixture of lacrosse, tennis and "bumble-puppy". They ran very fast on the special pelota "courts", light-footed in their espadrilles. My parents bought Robin and me some espadrilles and a basque beret each, which we wore all the time. We became so attached to our berets that we practically went to bed in them.

At some point on the journey we crossed over the Pamplona Gap, at the Roncevalles Pass, which I knew all about from a book of "heroes", telling of Roland's horn and his progress in the Pyrenees. We had to climb to a great height in our chugging hired car and kept stopping in case the engine boiled. The height affected my ears very badly and I lay in the bottom of the car with a rug over my head, seeing nothing of the journey. The twisty road also made me feel even sicker than before. But, in spite of all these misfortunes, I was always to say how much I had enjoyed our holiday and I am sure that this was true. The disagreeable part of a holiday is never remembered for very long, and one is usually left with a rosy picture of beautiful places visited and delicious meals enjoyed. I had been given a Box Brownie camera for my seventh birthday, so was able to stick my first very bad photographs of our holiday in my album. I was not to visit France and Spain again for nearly twenty years.

When Robin went back to school in the autumn of 1936, we packed up Chesley and set off, with Rogie, in the car to Scotland. This time, we were really going to live there FOREVER! (– well, as much as "forever" is ever possible for a sailor's family). My father would be leaving for China in a few weeks' time and he wanted to see us settled in, first.

My parents were in a great state of exhilaration. At last, everything they owned could come out of store, and they would have a home with which they could do exactly what they liked, instead of always having to remember that it did, in fact, belong to someone else. A great many of their wedding presents had been in store for nearly twelve years; now, at last, they could adorn their house with treasures they had not seen since their wedding day on 8th October 1924.

My mother loved gardening; it was in her blood. Several of her Hanbury forebears had been great gardeners, and one of them had created a famous garden, La Mortola, in Menton. Another had made a unique garden in Wester Ross, called Inverewe, which is now owned by the National Trust and welcomes visitors from all over the world. And a third had given the garden at Wisley to the Royal Horticultural Society. My mother used to say that, ever since she got married, she seemed to have been improving other people's gardens for them. Now she was to have one of her very own.

As we drove to Scotland, taking several days over the journey, as it always did in those days; and staying with friends on the way, my mother and father talked of all their exciting plans for Ardoch, the eighteenth-century house we had inherited near Glasgow. It was exactly what they wanted, they said, a smallish house set in a lovely big garden beside the great tidal river, where huge ships sailed down the Clyde to start on their voyage across the Atlantic.

I had only once been to Ardoch, from Lendrick in 1934, to visit my colourful great-uncle, "Don Roberto". I did not remember much about it, and all I knew about Scotland was connected with my much-loved Lendrick, a house that I loved almost as much as I loved Hitcham. I imagined Ardoch would be just like Lendrick and, I, too, was very excited. I was convinced there would be a large "Ben" or mountain behind the house, with heather and grouse, and little tinkling burns in which I could catch trout on a worm. I supposed there would also be a loch somewhere near with a boat to row, and lovely round stones with which to build dams and jetties. I hoped too that there might be a little fairy hill like the Drum, with bright green moss, red and white toadstools, and pale harebells with stems so slender that they hardly seemed able to hold up the bell at the top.

Looking back, it seems strange that my parents had not told me more about Ardoch before we went to live there. In those days, children were not treated to the endless explanations and careful psychology of the modern parent. We were just a part of the "luggage" that accompanied our parents through their early married life, and were taught to take life as it came. We were perfectly happy with this "no frills" approach to our upbringing, but life was full of surprises for us, to which it had not been thought necessary to condition us.

Ardoch was my biggest surprise of all. It was, in fact, an acute disappointment. I was too young to appreciate its architectural features: the oval drawing-room, thought to have been designed by one of the Adam brothers; the two miniature wings, each containing a perfect small room; the Adam mouldings on ceilings and doors; the walls covered with our ancestral portraits. To me, it was a small dark house, wedged between a road and a railway, and much too near the industrial sprawl that was Glasgow, which contained some of the worst slums in Britain.

The estate of Ardoch had been brought into the Graham family in the early eighteenth century by a marriage with an heiress, a Miss Bontine. Part of the terms of the entail decreed that the eldest son of a Graham of Gartmore must take the name Bontine while he was laird of Ardoch, until he inherited Gartmore, near Stirling, when he would change his name back to Graham.

My great uncle, "Don Roberto", had decided this was far too complicated, and merely added Bontine on to his own name; and my father was to do the same, in turn. In Uncle Robert's case he only had one christian name; but my father had three (one being obligatory, because King Edward VII was his godfather), so now that he had inherited Ardoch, his full names became Angus Edward Malise Bontine Cunninghame Graham, which had become a bit too much of a mouthful.

Gartmore had been sold by "Don Roberto" in 1900 to the Cayzer family, so we were never going to have to move from Ardoch, as our forebears had always done, to my mother's intense relief. But I was contrary enough, in my mood of disgruntlement to wish we could have lived at Gartmore, which was a large and beautiful mansion house near Stirling, set amongst picturesque hills, lochs and heather; or at another historic Graham house near Aberfoyle which I loved, called Duchray.

I was, of course, suffering from my "Englishness", in "real" Scotland, as I thought of it at that stage in my life. My idea of Scotland was still the romantic one of the English visitor to the Highlands; I was a child of the "six-week" wealthy English family who came to Scotland purely for the sport.

My own father had never been wealthy, and neither had his family before him. There had always been estates to be kept up, farm roofs to mend, fencing to repair, and improvements to be made to the many estate cottages. I was now beginning to learn what it was like to be truly Scottish, to be the daughter of a poorly paid Naval officer, who was also a Scottish laird. The two things made it unlikely that we should ever be able to contemplate living in the style of my Hanbury grandfather, with his profitable hop business, a reliable commodity always in demand by brewers.

But gradually I began to accept our new way of life, and to appreciate the rich and romantic history of my Scottish ancestors, whose portraits hung on our walls at Ardoch. I began to realise that this was my own special heritage. I also began to realise that to be Scottish meant absorbing Scotland "warts and all" – to love the country for its disasters and defeats as well as for its beauty and its "bonny purple heather".

I used to be told by my parents' friends that I had decidedly "Scottish" looks, and I had always been proud to be a Scot. Now I had the chance to prove that I should always care more about "the land of my fathers" than about the excitement of travel; although travelling, too, is a strong Scottish characteristic, which I was never to lose.

# CHAPTER X

— ◆ ——

**M**Y MOTHER RECEIVED her first letter from China in February 1937. My father wrote from Canton, where he had just arrived in his gunboat H.M.S. *Tarantula*.

"Today I got safely to my buoys here, though things rush at me from every direction, and if one sinks a sampan it is bound to have the entire family on board, all requiring compensation, not to mention all their savings for the past ten years."

Being captain of a small gunboat (less than 700 tons) on a Chinese river seemed at first to be a far more difficult job than being Commander of a light cruiser of around five thousand tons, such as the *Cardiff,* in South African waters. But my father was greatly enjoying his new life, and he was already seeing more of south China than many of the so-called "China hands" or taipans in Hong Kong had seen in a lifetime.

The reason for the continuing presence of foreign gunboats in Chinese rivers stemmed from the Treaty of Nanking in 1840, by which China received money and technical assistance from several western countries to help with the development of the country.

Having given this help, the countries involved wanted some return for it, so they started the International Chinese Customs Service, to take revenue from the resulting trade on the Yangtze and West Rivers and at various treaty ports on the coast.

This led to customs posts on the larger rivers, and also to concessions of land on which the foreign traders and those supervising the working of the Treaty could live. (In Canton, the concession was the Island of Shameen.) The Treaty also insisted on gunboats from each nation being allowed on the two big rivers to see that the terms of the Treaty were kept, and to protect the foreigners who were involved in trading and supervising.

The Chinese merchants and farmers who lived near the rivers were in constant fear of piracy and banditry, so they welcomed these foreign gunboats. They did not trust their own Chinese officers, for they were quite likely to be naval officers one day and pirates the next. Chiang Kai-shek and his followers were totally against having foreign gunboats on the rivers of China, but most of the responsible Chinese knew that they could not protect their own people from piracy unless the ships remained, and were to continue to patrol their rivers.

I think my father felt his role was genuinely to help to look after the Chinese, and to smooth the way for their own enterprises. He did not feel he was acting as a "policeman" or a "Customs officer". He was unconsciously following in the footsteps of his great-great-uncle Mountstuart Elphinstone, whose attitude to India had been very similar. Neither of them were ever to feel superior or patronising towards the race they had come to live amongst. They were genuinely trying to help them to develop their own countries. My father came to love the Chinese, although he was well aware that there would always be a streak of indifference, perhaps even cruelty, in their natures. Because they always took such a long view, even of everyday events, what we might call cruelty would, to the Chinese, always seem to be "a step in the right direction". Drowning baby girls at birth was at that time the only way they could think of achieving, quite literally, "birth control". The recent massacres after student risings in our own day are probably considered an unpleasant necessity to ensure future stability for their country.

An example of my father's genuine courtesy to the Chinese is shown quite unselfconsciously in a letter he wrote from Canton a few days after the first one, on 19th February 1937.

"I created a precedent by calling on the Chinese Commissioner of Customs, who was pleased as he had not been called on before, there being some idea that he should call first.

"This I considered rubbish as he is of equal standing with the mayor, on whom I would certainly call. Our gunboats all use his Customs Club for recreation, it is his country, and anyhow, no 'face' can ever be lost by common civility. He was a nice old boy of the old school, though outwardly one cannot tell what Chinese are like inside and I have no doubt he would cheerfully torture one if he had the chance. We did much bowing and exchanging of murmured compliments in the approved style; he promised to be the lifelong friend of me and the gunboats and accepted an invitation to lunch on board next time I came in.

"I am now off to a place on the way to Macau *(a)* to find a passage which is supposed to be tricky, and *(b)* to see if the snipe and duck reputed to be there really exist."

There were many tricky passages in the West River, but my father was determined to find out for himself how tricky they really were.

"I am not prepared to send gunboats to places I hesitate to go to myself and the river pilotage cannot be kept up to the mark unless slight risks are taken. I don't call sitting on a sandbank a risk as I have only to call up the rest of the gunboats to come and tow me off. I tell you all this so that you will know, if you hear that the *Tula* is high and dry in a paddy field, that at any rate I shall not feel I have 'lost face'."

Another letter from my father about his activities in *Tula* (the Chinese crew's name for *Tarantula*) showed that sometimes the risks were rather greater than "just sitting on a sandbank". He found that a small place called Sam Shui had Europeans living there and therefore it was important to know if the gunboats could get there in an emergency. This meant negotiating two hairpin bends, dodging a submerged rock and finally sailing within ten yards of the riverbank to avoid a shoal. All this had to be done at about eight knots to avoid losing steerage way owing to the fast current; there was also the problem of the water mark, which in places was at minus one foot six, zero being the usual lowest reading.

It appeared that no gunboat had attempted to get to Sam Shui in living memory, so my father was determined to break the "bad joss", which he fortunately managed to do "by a certain amount of good fortune, and by being rather rough with the helm".

While my father was learning his job as Senior Naval Officer, West River, and with respites in Hong Kong for more social activities, we had been settling in to Ardoch. Because we now knew that we should probably join my father in China within the year, my mother rightly or wrongly decided against sending me to the excellent girls' school in the nearby town of Helensburgh, called St. Bride's. She had never gone to school herself, receiving her education at home from a series of governesses, so it never occurred to her that this might now be somewhat old-fashioned. Neither did she realise that I would be excessively isolated from children of my own age, if I did not go to a proper school. In her case, there had always been much coming and going at Hitcham, with an elder brother, two elder sisters, and with her younger brother constantly as a close companion.

In my case, I was alone far too much of the time, which was why I read so much and invented imaginary companions. I know that I should have loved to have gone to school at this time, because I was really rather sociable, although perfectly capable of entertaining myself on my own.

It also meant that I never got to know the children in my own neighbourhood at Ardoch, except when we were all on our best behaviour at birthday parties, to which I was sometimes asked, or at the weekly dancing class at the Victoria Hall in Helensburgh, to which I went. Because I did not know my contemporaries as a child, I was later to feel that I had always been an "outsider" in that part of Scotland and never "one of them".

No parent can possibly get everything right in the upbringing of their children, and I am sure that my mother felt the advantages of having a governess far outweighed the disadvantages. I could continue with my lessons on the six-week sea voyage by P&O, and more important still, my mother could always feel that I had a responsible grown-up to look after me in a foreign country, if she needed to be away on occasions with my father. From her point of view, it was undoubtedly the right answer, but I still doubt if it was for me.

Miss Gibson arrived at Ardoch in the autumn of 1936, shortly after my father had left for China. She was Scottish, a reserved Borderer, and a very different type to my cosy, talkative Nanny. But she had a good sense of humour and she was a first class teacher, with original ideas of her own. I suspect she also understood me very well; and, was quite ready to join in my "imaginings" with me, to my surprise and delight. But she was also strict, and often unresponsive, and I never felt I really knew her well. I am sure I relied on her greatly and was happy to be with her, but unlike the great love I had for Nanny, this was one based more on mutual respect than on deep affection.

There are two photographs taken at this time of Miss Gibson and me, sitting beside a genial looking chimpanzee at the London Zoo who had been taught to put his arm round "the customers" for the photograph. In the photograph Miss Gibson is sitting very straight and holding herself away from the chimpanzee's embrace, with an embarrassed smile. In mine, I have turned towards the chimp with a look of great love, my hand curled confidingly in his. These two photos say a great deal about us both; perhaps Miss Gibson's reaction was the more normal one, but I was longing for friendship, even from a chimpanzee.

We sent the photographs to my grandfather and he wrote me a charming letter saying "I like the one of you and your mother very much, but how she has changed since I last saw her!".

The Coronation of King George VI and Queen Elizabeth took place in the early summer of 1937. As a child, I don't remember being particularly aware of the unhappy events that had preceded it, although the name "Mrs Simpson" had been on everyone's lips, and all the grown-ups talked about her in derogatory tones.

My father's own comment about it was "A sad affair, but well handled under great difficulty by Baldwin. Edward VIII was so likeable, as I found when we were boys, and when I was a sub-lieutenant in the Royal Yacht. He had many qualities, but lacked the one essential for a king – good judgement." My father had seen a good deal of the two young princes when his family used to be lent a house at Balmoral while his father was "in waiting" to King George V.

Another personal connection for our family resulted from the King's abdication, in favour of his younger brother. My uncle, Admiral Sir Basil Brooke, married to my father's only sister, had been controller of the Duke of York's household and he was made Private Secretary to Duchess of York, now the new Queen Elizabeth. Because of this we were invited to the great Royal Naval Review at Portsmouth, which was to take place on my birthday. Sadly for me, I caught a 'flu virus, and had to spend my birthday in bed instead. It was the most miserable day of my life. Indeed, I felt very jealous of my mother and my brother, and very sorry for myself.

For the Coronation itself, my mother was given special tickets for the stands that had been erected in the London streets. She and Robin were, once more, to go to the forecourt of Buckingham Palace, and Miss Gibson and I went to a stand beside the Admiralty. I think we probably had the best view, right up the Mall to Buckingham Palace. We had been living in our London house, and I can remember a sleepless night because of the noise of metal crowd-barriers being installed in the streets. Next morning, we had to get up very early and walk from Elizabeth Street to the Mall, because most of the streets were closed to traffic. We then sat for what seemed like hours before we saw the great gold coach bearing the King and his Queen to their Coronation at Westminster Abbey.

But there was plenty to keep us interested, as the important guests and the foreign kings and queens, and heads of state, streamed between the crowded stands in their coaches, with lines of smart sailors on guard in front of our part of the procession, because we were in front of the Admiralty.

In London there are always plenty of wags who make funny remarks on these occasions and there were several in our stand to keep us amused by their wit. When a dustman went past from time to time to sweep up the horses' droppings, there was always a huge cheer from the crowd. Afterwards, I wrote a short poem about it all:

"When I went to the Coronation
 I found a new occupation
 It was to count the sailors' hats
 Which looked like lots of snowy cats.
 But when the coach did come along
 I found that I was very wrong
 For they became like hats once more
 And I could count them, score on score."

I think, probably, even more than the quick glimpse of the King and Queen, and the two delightful little princesses (one being two years older than me, and the other a year younger), my greatest and most vivid memory was of the enormous crowds of people who gathered in London for the memorable occasion.

In the evening, we joined a happy throng in St. James's Park, to watch a firework display. There were thousands of people there, all good humoured and enjoying the event. We never heard of crowd "problems" in those days. But I do remember being somewhat alarmed, that night, in the park, as we were engulfed in waves of people, and I clung tightly to my mother and Miss Gibson and Robin.

Eventually, a large man, with his own family in tow, helped to carve a way through the crowd for us, at the end of the firework display, calling out in a jolly voice, "Follow father! Follow father! Gently does it!". We could just see his head above the crowds as he weaved his way, with us following behind.

Meanwhile, my father was celebrating the Coronation in Canton at the same time, with his flotilla of four gunboats playing an important part. He described it all in a letter to my mother.

"We manned and cheered ship at noon and I gather my silvery voice ordering the Flotilla cheers was heard all over the Pearl River and most of the province of Kwangtung. After which we 'spliced the main brace'. Later in the day the gunboats gave a party and a fireworks display which was much enjoyed by the Chinese, who had, after all, originally invented fireworks, and they are still their great passion.

"By dint of much wireless practice, all four ships suddenly appeared out of the darkness completely floodlit, and shortly afterwards, eighty red, white and blue rockets went off together in one bouquet, followed by a short searchlight display during which the lights concentrated on the British Consulate's large silk flag. Finally, more rockets, and another simultaneous floodlighting display, which was kept on so that the guests, and the Chinese in Canton, could enjoy the floodlit scene.

"It was particularly effective, with the ships painted white; and as the French Consul (with his national picturesque phrasing), said, 'It was as though an invisible hand had suddenly painted the ships on a blackboard.'

"Two Chinese generals standing next to me gave out spontaneous 'Hiya's' and involuntarily clapped their hands in front of their stout tums."

"So you see, we *really* 'coronated'!" he ended his letter. The Chinese had enjoyed the celebrations just as much as the loyal subjects of the new King Emperor, King George VI.

My father's letters from China had been so full of information that they helped us to know what to expect of our new life, before my mother and I and Miss Gibson sailed on board the P&O ship *Ranchi* at the end of September 1937.

# CHAPTER XI

O UR TRIP OUT TO China was memorable for me. I had
recently celebrated my ninth birthday, so I was at
exactly the right age to take it all in, and to enjoy every
moment. I remember being fully aware of how lucky I was.

We said our sad farewells to Robin, who was going to
Lendrick with my grandparents for his summer holidays.
Fortunately he was looking forward greatly to being with his
cousins, Bill and John, again, and he did not seem at all upset by
our departure. It has to be remembered that it was much more
normal in those days to leave a boy at school in England, and he
probably felt rather superior about it. He would soon be going
to Dartmouth and it would only be five years till he would
become a midshipman; at which point in his Naval career he
might well be parted from his family for several years on end
after going to sea. We all accepted the parting as a fact of life.
Robin was shortly coming up to his twelfth birthday, and a boy
of twelve in the 1930's was considered to be very nearly adult.
I am always surprised when I hear my friends saying "My
children are far more grown-up at twelve than I was". I,
personally, do not find this to be true, partly, I believe, because
they spend far more time with their parents nowadays, so they
do not have to be nearly so self-reliant or responsible. Also, to
be fair, with the crime rate increasing year by year, it is unwise
for present-day parents to allow their children to travel by

themselves, something we did quite normally after the age of twelve in my own childhood, especially if our parents were sailors or soldiers.

We sailed on 24th September 1937 and our first port of call was Marseilles. I had read *The Man in the Iron Mask* and was longing to see Chateau d'If. It was very hot in Marseilles, so we did not do much sightseeing there, but I remember the great white Notre-Dame-de-la-Garde on the Plateau de la Croix as we sailed into the harbour in the *Ranchi*.

Several more passengers came on board in Marseilles. For those who suffered badly from sea-sickness, it was much more pleasant to travel by train overland to the south of France to join the ship, rather than being tossed about in the Bay of Biscay. Once we got into the Mediterranean, instead of hot soup for our elevenses, we were given ice-cream. The next stop was Malta and I was fascinated by the dahaisas with their high prows and the women wearing black capes which formed a wide hood over their heads to protect them from the sun. My mother was thrilled to see the island again.

After Malta, we did not stop again until we reached Port Said at the start of the Suez Canal. I did lessons every morning with Miss Gibson, and she had taught me about De Lesseps who built the canal and whose statue stands at the entrance to it. At Port Said, the "gully-gully" man came on board the *Ranchi*, and conjured baby chickens out of the toes of my sandals. I was enchanted by him. When he pulled a chicken out of Miss Gibson's ear, she gave a shudder and went very pink.

Now, at last, we were approaching "the east" and I felt a new sort of magic creeping over me. It was not the more obvious magic of the "gully-gully" man, but something that seemed to fill my whole mind and my body with a throbbing excitement and mystery, delicious new scents in the air, the hubbub of chattering Egyptians and Arabs, the bright colours of their clothes and tarbooshes and the gold necklaces and bracelets in their markets and down tiny winding streets in the souks.

I saw camels for the first time and marvelled at their swift movements, their bodies looking so clumsy and awkward. Miss Gibson and I went to the great store, or bazaar, called Simon Artz, and I bought a little leather purse with camels and square-looking ancient Egyptians tooled on it. I have it to this day.

I remember the *Ranchi*'s progress down the Suez Canal. The ship seemed to take up the whole canal; and, after being at sea, it was strange to be moving along at what seemed like walking pace, accompanied by men in flowing garments and their camels trudging along beside us. Perhaps the canal is far wider than I can remember, but this was my own impression at the time.

Aden was nothing but bare rocks ("The barren Rocks of Aden", that famous pipe tune) and intense heat. I felt sorry for the soldiers and their families who were stationed at this important strategic point of the defence of the British Empire and the gateway to the east.

Then we were out into "the pink Arabian sea", as Kipling so aptly described it. The magic increased, and I can vividly remember our arrival at Bombay. We sailed in very early in the morning and the whole scene was pink mist, rather like a pantomime set looked at through a pink chiffon curtain in the "transformation scene". Gradually, the burning sun began to rise, and suddenly I saw India.

This was the highest point of the whole sea voyage for me. There was something about that tiny corner of India that showed me a new and magical world. I can understand perfectly why India was such a strong magnetic force for the British through the ages. It was everything that Britain is not: throngs of friendly people, continuous heat which caused a feeling of pleasurable languor; exotic fruit and flowers; and sacred cows wandering in the streets. There was the other side as well, of course, the poverty, the maimed beggars, and the malnutrition.

We are now used to seeing Indians and Pakistanis in our own streets, but they make me feel very unhappy because they are totally out of their own environment, and have lost all their vibrant colour and their happy way of life. It was the people themselves that made India such a fascinating country: their kindness, their gentleness, their intelligence and their immense generosity, whatever their station or situation in life.

How was I able to feel all this in two days in Bombay, I wonder? There is always something extraordinarily vivid about a first impression: the longer you stay in a country, the more this original understanding is lost, because, unconsciously, you begin to force something of your own outlook upon it, and gradually you become less receptive to the influences of the country. I did not have time to be "me" in Bombay. I was, instead, swirled into the permanently moving force, paradoxically so still at its heart, which was India.

Years later, I was to visit Delhi, where I saw Lutyen's memorable triumphal arch, which is totally unadorned apart from the word "India". I was not only breathtakingly impressed by it, but there was something very familiar about it. I have only recently discovered that in Bombay there is an exact replica of this archway, which I must have seen when I was nine years old. The gateway to India.

My mother was invited to take us to Government House for lunch (or was it to Admiralty House?). All I can remember was the grandeur, and the slowly swaying punkahs in the dining-room, as we ate mango ice. (Another of my "taste memories".)

I suspect my mother was taken on a sightseeing tour after lunch by our hosts, who by then had had enough of "the governess and the child" (which was a perfectly normal attitude in those days). Unbelievably, Miss Gibson and I went to a huge airy cinema where we saw a Shirley Temple film! An incongruous way of spending an afternoon in Bombay.

After the film was over, Miss Gibson and I just had time to plunge into one of the seething bazaars where I bought some cheap silver bracelets with my pocket money. As I only got 6d a week, they must have been very cheap indeed. Then, back on board the *Ranchi* to our cabin which had become "home'.

From Bombay, we sailed down the coast of India to Ceylon, now called Sri Lanka. We went on an expedition inland from Colombo and I remember silent Singhalese men, women and children, walking quietly along shady roads, and large elephants carrying heavy loads. My new world was becoming more exotic day by day, and I was enchanted by it. Most of all, I remember the smells. The heavy scent of frangipani, the lush smells of undergrowth after tropical rain, the smells of human and animal excretion, everything mixed together quite naturally to produce that astonishing odour that is "abroad", and especially "abroad in the tropics".

For those who have lived many years in tropical countries, I believe our own country also has a distinctive smell. I shall never forget the way my son, who had been in Venezuela for eight years, put his head out of the car window sniffing the Scottish countryside delightedly, as we bowled along, on his first return visit, exclaiming "Mum, does Scotland always smell like this?". He, too, has inherited my strong memory through smell, and on turning the pages of a childhood photograph book, he sees himself aged ten, setting out to go fishing and says "I can remember exactly what that anorak *smelt* like!".

Penang was even more beautiful than Colombo. Now we were in Malaya and we saw quantities of small brown monkeys in the parks and gardens. But there was a sadness for me in Penang. Several of the families on board ship were going to Malaya, including my best friend amongst the children on that voyage, Felicity Anne. We had played together all the way from England, and had become inseparable. At children's meals we always sat next to each other, and we used to love to run round the decks together greeting the members of the crew who had become our special friends.

Life on board a P&O steamship was very like life in a large country house. The children were kept quite separate from the grown-ups and our lives hardly touched. We had our meals at different times and ate with our nannies and governesses. The few mothers who were going to join their husbands and were looking after their own children on the voyage also ate with us. Our food was quite different to the grown-up passengers' food as I was shortly to discover. And, just as it had been at Hitcham, our real friends amongst the adults were the stewards and the stewardesses, the crew, and the younger and less exalted ship's officers. We were allowed almost anywhere we liked in the ship, except in the 1st Class, and wherever we roamed, there was always a kind sailor or steward to keep an eye on us. As far as I know, no child has ever been lost overboard from a P&O ship. I remember asking our steward where the milk came from: "Oh, we have a tin cow below" he said. From that moment, I was quite convinced that the tin cow was milked every morning and night, and I repeatedly asked to be allowed to watch the milking, but was firmly told it was not allowed. I longed to see that tin cow, and went on asking till the last day of the voyage, but was completely unsuccessful.

There had been a party for the children on the voyage out, but I had not enjoyed it much because I was suffering from the heat – we were sailing through the Red Sea – and had developed a large boil on my backside. I remember having anti-flogistine slapped on my bottom, and sitting in a basin of hot water with epsom salts in it (or was it bicarbonate of soda?) to draw the boil. My dignity was severely dented. I attended the party, but unfortunately one of the rougher boys gave me a kick up the backside and caught me on the tender spot, which was so painful that I nearly passed out. From my point of view, the children's party was not a success.

Nevertheless I was sad when the children had all left the ship, their families being mainly tea planters from Ceylon or rubber planters from Malaya, I was back to my more normal solitary state, and I missed Felicity Anne, but I soon began to enjoy being the only child on board the *Ranchi,* as we sailed on down the Strait of Malacca to Singapore. Best of all, children's meals were now cancelled and Miss Gibson and I were allowed to eat with my mother. The meals were not only at more civilised hours (lunch at 1 o'clock instead of 12), but the food was out of this world. Being a greedy child, as has already become apparent, I enjoyed the final part of the trip quite enormously.

Another curious thing about those final days on board the *Ranchi* was that friends of my mother's, who she had made on the voyage, suddenly started to take notice of me, and were very friendly and kind. I suppose it was natural for the adult passengers to pay little attention to the children on board when we went about in a noisy gang. I expect we were tiresome and rude, en masse; on our own we were much more polite, and even ready to enjoy the company of our parents' friends, who we had previously thought were boring and stuffy.

We sailed on, with Sumatra on our starboard bow, and with soft winds blowing spicy scents offshore. Then we arrived at Singapore. We were to stay in port for at least two days in Singapore. The *Ranchi* must have had a good deal of cargo to unload and probably some minor repairs to be undertaken before setting out in the rough China Sea, with its risk of typhoons.

# CHAPTER XII

———————◆◆◆———————

THERE HAD ALREADY been a serious typhoon in China at the beginning of September, and we received my father's description of it when we arrived in Singapore.

"The typhoon which did so much damage in Hong Kong, and about which you must have read, came on to me at Kongmun (just south of Pearl River) with practically undiminished fury and gave me the most anxious and strenuous nine hours that I have ever spent on the bridge of a ship.

"We had a warning during the day and as I had intended anchoring nearer the mouth of the river, I quickly turned and ran back for Kongmun, which was less unsuitable.

"We arrived just after dark, having had two violent rain squalls on the way. By this time we had all our awnings furled, topmast housed, loose gear secure, a good scope of cable to ride by, and steam up. I then went to bed not expecting to have very long in it and, sure enough, was called at 2.15 am with news that it was beginning to blow and that the full force typhoon signal had been hoisted at Hong Kong.

"By 3.15 it was blowing a full gale down the river from the northwest and to try to steady the ship from yawing, I let go the second anchor, which proved of little use.

"Soon after 4 am, it was obvious we were beginning to drag, so, rather than start towing anchors round the river, I got the cable party to weigh them, in spite of it being most difficult to stand up as the gusts were getting to over a 100 miles per hour.

"Having got under way, the fun really began. It was still dark, deluging rain and blowing such as I have never seen it (at Hong Kong it was estimated as 150 miles per hour).

"The river at Kongmun is pear-shaped with the stalk up-river. My chief concern was to keep the gunboat in the wide part, but this was made very difficult owing to the fact that in order to keep the ship manageable (she is like a sort of floating cake tin), it was necessary to forge ahead upstream. The further up I got, the less room there was to manoeuvre. An attempt to turn her by going ahead nearly drove us into a formidable collection of wooden and concrete piles for a jetty. I went full speed astern and anxiously watched for the bow to retreat from the piles, which it did all too slowly, hitting one large wooden one which was luckily rotten and did no damage.

"The wind was still just as strong but it was going round fast through north towards east, and the veering of the wind meant that I could now hold the ship stern to wind and allow the current to take her down, out of the narrow port which I was continually trying to avoid. I spent the next six hours steering round and round and up and down in this restricted area like a clockwork boat in a bath, making frequent unsuccessful attempts to anchor. By 5.30 am it was mercifully beginning to get light, which made the rest of the proceedings a little less difficult. It wasn't until 11.45 am that the wind had moderated sufficiently to get an anchor to hold, and I was able to leave the bridge for the first time to get something to eat.

"It was, no doubt, a very good experience, but I do not particularly want it repeated.

"By 3.00 pm the wind had quite gone and I landed to see the havoc ashore."

The Chinese-Japanese war was by now beginning to escalate in northern China, and on 7th September, after describing the terrors of the typhoon, my father ended his letter by saying:

"There is still nothing to stop you coming, and if anything by some unlikely chance crops up, you can always go to Ceylon, where I believe there is a very good hotel up in the hills in a lovely climate."

Obviously, this was not going to be necessary, although interestingly enough, the "Good hotel up in the hills" in Ceylon, mentioned by my father, was to be very near the Governor's summer residence, Peredina, close to Kandy, where Mountbatten established his luxurious headquarters as Supreme Commander of the South East Asia Command (S.E.A.C.) in the Second World War, having moved it from New Delhi.

The two days in Singapore were happy ones for my mother, Miss Gibson and me. We were made temporary members of a Country Club for British families where there was a huge swimming pool in which we basked and kept cool. The heat was intense and extremely humid, so the pool was the best place to be. On the rare occasions we came out of the water, we sat in bamboo chairs sipping fresh iced lime juice, while fans swung round on the ceilings of the huge airy rooms.

I also remember being given something delicious to eat called an "Eskimo Pie", which I have always thought was the perfect name for an ice-cream.

Then, on we sailed through the China Seas, which were surprisingly calm on that voyage, towards our final destination, Hong Kong.

# CHAPTER XIII

———————◆◆◆———————

OUR HOME IN Hong Kong was half way up the Peak, at Garden Terrace. We were quite close to the lowest station of the Peak Tram. Garden Terrace might easily have stood in Glasgow or Edinburgh, or even Bath. The solid early nineteenth century houses were stone built and beautifully cool. We had a first floor flat, which was just as big as the original late eighteenth-century flats built in the Georgian houses of Edinburgh's New Town. We also had a superb view over Hong Kong harbour.

The taipans, who were the important British businessmen in Hong Kong (not to be confused with the sampans, as my father used to joke), lived at the top of the Peak in sumptuous houses, which I saw from time to time when I was invited to their children's birthday parties.

Hong Kong society in those days (and probably to this day) was a meritocracy. Everyone had risen to the top of his profession through his own skills and qualities. My father, as Senior Naval Officer, West River, and a Captain in the Royal Navy, tended to make friends with the executive chiefs of the old established British Trading Companies like Jardine Matheson, and Butterfield & Swire, and also with the Consul General, Palliser (whose son was, after the Second World War, to become head of the Foreign Office). He also made friends with the Commodore of the Dockyard, and the Colonel of the

Seaforth Highlanders, the regiment which was based in Hong Kong at the time. On board the *Tarantula*, my father had a bowl of beautiful Chinese goldfish in his dining-cabin, and they were all called after the Hong Kong "taipans" – Jardine, Matheson, Butterfield, Swire, etc. etc. – which always helped to break the ice when he gave a party!

In addition, there was a very cosmopolitan society of "refugees", especially White Russians, who had fled to Hong Kong after the 1917 horror in their own country, with whom we made friends. My ballet teacher was a White Russian and he tried to turn us all into budding Pavlovas, becoming very angry when he realised that the material he had been given to work on had absolutely no potential. We had to lie on our fronts on the floor, grasping our ankles with our hands, until our toes touched the backs of our heads. Very few English children are the right shape for this elegant exercise at the age of nine or ten, and he must have despaired when he looked at our plump little bodies, so lacking in natural Russian grace.

"I vill put my arm srough ze hoop you make wiz ze body, like so," he would announce, showing what he intended to do by using the one beautiful little Russian girl in our class as his model. (Perhaps of all of us, she was his one success? Perhaps she did become a prima ballerina in the end? Or did she end up in Stanley Prison Camp like so many of our friends?)

The Russian ballet master would then approach each one of us in turn to swing us up and off the ground. It was agony hanging on to our ankles, knowing that he meant what he said when he shouted angrily at us, "I vill drop you if you let go ze ankles!"

There were three families who were my particular friends. There were the Dibleys, an engineer rear admiral with a family of four daughters and one baby son, called Jan, Sue, Nan, Prue and Hugh; the Blacks, one of the shipping families, who had two daughters called Vera and Elizabeth; and a doctor's family who lived close by, the Durrands, who happened to be related to our Scottish lawyer, Mr Hunter, of Bonar, Hunter & Johnstone.

Because I did not go to the one big European girls' school on the island, I had very few close friends in Hong Kong. It was just the same as it had been at Ardoch; at children's parties I was the outsider, "that girl who does lessons with her governess". I felt rather like a spaniel that had got into a pack of hounds by mistake.

The children's parties were fun if they were properly organised by the grown-ups; but if they were not, then they inevitably turned into a battle between the boys and the girls. We girls were at the "I hate boys" age, and they in turn, felt exactly the same way about us.

I don't remember really knowing any boys in Hong Kong, except the Durrand boy, and one little mouse of a boy called Michael, younger than me, who came to do lessons with me because he had been ill and was not strong enough to go to school. He was very gentle, with a shy smile, and I grew rather fond of him.

The girl I enjoyed being with most of all was Jan Dibley. Her big family quickly realised how lonely I was, and often took me off on their own jolly expeditions. Sometimes we went in their sailing boat to one of the smaller islands to swim and picnic. On one occasion, I was swimming off the boat in deep water when I panicked and started to sink. With great presence of mind Jan, who swam like a fish, managed to grab me and pull me to the safety of their boat. I was still a very inadequate swimmer and swimming out of my depth always frightened me. I remember thinking that Jan, at barely ten-years-old, had quite probably saved me from drowning. She was always to be a calm practical person, and our friendship continued to grow as we found ourselves ultimately at the same schools in England, and later still, as godparents of each other's children.

Most of my parents' friends lived on top of the Peak, but we much preferred being only half way up, because their houses were frequently shrouded in thick mist when the clouds were low. Our lovely view of Victoria and the harbour was nearly always clear, and the most exciting moment of all was when we saw my father's gunboat, H.M.S. *Tarantula,* sailing into the harbour from one of her many excursions up the West River to Canton, her white paint gleaming, and the white ensign straining out from her stern in the breeze.

Our servants were Chinese and I was to grow very fond of them. (Just as I had loved Gertrude, or "Rosebud" in South Africa.) We did not need a proper children's amah, but we had a delightful "Wash Amah". She was small and neat in her black silk trousers and blue top, with a long black plait down her back. She walked with a hobbling motion, because her feet had been bound as a child. This was a cruel custom, now thankfully stopped, when a baby's feet were bound so that they would never grow, tiny feet being considered a Chinese woman's greatest asset.

Our "Number One Boy" was called Ah Tsu, a tall good-looking young man with beautiful manners.

On board *Tarantula* my father had a devoted Chinese servant called Ah Lo, and a driver called Ah Choy. One day, my father was looking through a drawer in his cabin and was astonished to find that it contained two white shirts, three pairs of stockings, two dirty vests, six cartridges, a packet of candles, and a pair of riding breeches. Ah Lo was given a sound ticking off and made to put the shirts all in one drawer, vests in another, cartridges in the magazine and candles in the store; with the result that my father was satisfied and Ah Lo could find nothing.

The Chinese mind does not work on these lines. But the most important and valuable quality of the Chinese servant is his willingness to do the job well. He does not feel that he is being "put upon", so he carries out his duties with intense professional pride.

My father remembered once getting dressed to go to an important Chinese dinner. Ah Lo had all his clothes pressed and laid out, and helped to get my father ready to go. An hour or so later, during the banquet, there was a tap on my father's shoulder and there, amongst the many Chinese servants waiting at table, was Ah Lo standing quietly behind his chair.

"Master forget cigalette case. I bling it" he whispered, handing my father his silver case. Ah Lo had walked nearly two miles to the function to bring something he knew his Master would need, which had been left behind. This showed his complete dedication.

Chinese servants are apt to take things literally, as my mother and I discovered one day when we went for a shopping expedition "down town" with the driver, Ah Choy, to take us in the car.

The best shops were in a rabbit warren of tiny narrow streets near the Star Ferry, and as the car was no help to us once we got there, my mother dismissed Ah Choy, asking him to come back to meet us an hour later. We emerged with our parcels at the appointed hour and there was Ah Choy standing waiting for us.

"Where is the car?" my mother asked, thinking he must have parked it somewhere else. "Me not bling car," beamed Ah Choy, "Missy say 'meet me in one hour', so I come, like she say."

My mother and I were hard put to it not to burst out laughing. Ah Choy never did understand what he had done wrong but he found us a rickshaw and ran beside us on the long, hot trail up to Garden Terrace.

Once a week I had a French lesson from an enormously fat French lady of uncertain age who arrived at Garden Terrace in a sedan chair. We all used rickshaws quite normally in those days, but very few people used sedan chairs.

I used to watch the coolies trudging up the zig-zagging road to Garden Terrace, with the enormous lady bulging over the sides of the carrying chair like a huge pink blancmange. When she got to our door, she used to climb out of the chair with great difficulty, mopping the sweat from her brow with a small scented lace handkerchief. I was never quite sure why she was so hot, after all, she hadn't walked a step. It was the coolies I was really sorry for. She was so fat and unattractive that I could not take my eyes off her, and therefore learnt very little French from her.

117

My father had recently experienced rather the same trouble trying to learn Cantonese. His teacher from Canton was an old man with a large wart on his face, out of which sprouted at least eight very long hairs. My father was riveted by this phenomenon, of which his teacher was obviously proud, and he found it impossibly distracting. He admitted later that he did not think he could have learnt Cantonese in any case, in the short time he had to spare from his Naval duties, because it was a very complicated language. There were at least fifty vowel sounds to learn, and each one had to be said in six different tones, so that the smallest mistake in the tone turned it into a completely different word. (T'ong at the highest pitch meant "Chinese", and T'ong at the lowest pitch meant "to kill".)

My greatest treat of all was to be given a few "tickies", as we called the small change, and to be allowed to go by myself down our zig-zagging road to the Peak tram station where a flower-seller sat. For the equivalent of around 6d, I would buy a huge basket of gladioli for my mother. It wasn't so much the idea of giving my mother flowers that appealed to me, as much as the short unaccompanied walk amongst the Chinese, during which I felt able to identify with them in a way that was impossible when I was in tow with my very British parents and governess. I have probably inherited the love of travel that was so important to my great uncle "Don Roberto" Cunninghame Graham. Not just "seeing places", but getting in amongst the people, to feel a part of them.

I must have had this instinct at a very early age, for, even at the age of nine in Hong Kong, I remember being horrified at the way the Chinese were treated by some of the British ex-patriates. I loved that walk to the flower-seller and was probably quite unaware that Miss Gibson was supervising every inch of my progress from a window in our flat above. I suppose I should not have been allowed to go by myself, if she had not been able to keep me in sight throughout my short expedition.

Best of all, as winter approached, I loved to see the little round padded Chinese toddlers in their colourful quilted coats and fur-lined boots. They looked like small rubber balls with beaming faces. It got quite cold in mid-winter, which I had not expected, and it was definitely "jersey-and-skirt" weather, rather than "cotton-frock" weather.

Sometimes on my walks I would see flocks of bright green parakeets fly screeching into the trees. I remember someone saying they came from Australia, which seemed an astonishing piece of information to me.

I often wished I was allowed to walk alone in what I called "the Chinese streets" as opposed to the "British streets" where we lived. The Chinese lived in unbelievable squalor, in narrow streets where the sewage ran down the gutters. The smell was appalling, but to me it was all a part of the fascination of Hong Kong. The children were dressed very colourfully, but the adult Chinese wore black trousers and blue tops for the most part, both men and women. Every house had its bird cage, with a small brown bird singing tunefully. The older members of the family were deeply revered and on the street outside their houses there was nearly always a group of old men playing mahjong, with loud and incessant clicking of the tiles, which they moved so quickly that it looked like sleight of hand.

There was always something to watch in those streets, especially if you could peep into the little pitch dark craftsmen's houses, where they were carving ivory balls that fitted, inexplicably, one inside the other; or beautiful jade figures of men and animals.

Best of all were the tiny porcelain figures which I used to buy with my "tickies", old men complete with straggly beards and hairy warts on their faces, like my father's Chinese teacher. There were black and white Chinese pigs with families of piglets or walkie ducks, which we used to see herded about by small boys when we went to the mainland, and there were also replicas, in miniature, of Chinese bowls and vases with scenes of spiky mountains, or ladies in flowing kimonos. I soon had quite a collection of these small objects, which I suppose would be quite valuable today, although I never paid more than a shilling (my total wealth at any one time) for any of them.

Once, we were lucky enough to see the famous dragon-boat race. The boats were long and narrow, with a dragon's figurehead as a prow, holding about seventy paddlers who, encouraged by a man with a large drum to give the time, got the boats along at the most amazing pace. My father was to comment afterwards that this was one of their means of reducing the population, since hardly any of the Chinese could swim, so drownings during the race were frequent. Apparently, it was also the traditional moment to settle old scores, so apart from the "accidental" drownings during the race, many Chinese were bumped off in subsequent fights after the race between rival villages. (The Chinese version of football hooliganism, I suppose.)

Because of the living conditions of two-thirds of the population of Hong Kong at the time we were there, there were apt to be cholera and typhoid scares, so we were never allowed to drink the water. All our water was thoroughly boiled and kept in bottles with screw tops in a large white enamel "ice-box", about the size of a freezer chest. We were not even allowed to clean our teeth in tap water, and I can remember thinking how marvellous it would be when we got home again to use my toothbrush under a running tap.

All our fruit and vegetables were washed in boiled water, and our ice-cream was made at home with pasteurised milk and cream. We were never allowed to buy ice-creams or soft drinks from stalls or shops.

For me, this produced one real difficulty. If I went with my parents to a place where the grown-ups ordered drinks from a bar, I was not allowed to have a soft drink or even water. (Strangely enough, I don't believe bottled mineral water existed in Hong Kong in those days.) I was allowed fizzy drinks, but at that age I disliked them intensely, so I had to go thirsty.

Eventually, my father took the matter in hand with his usual common-sense. He knew I loved to come and watch him play polo, so he announced that in the future, I could only come if I drank a whole glass of fizzy lemonade during the match. Naturally I agreed to his terms and (as he had fully expected) I soon grew to like fizzy lemonade after all. I have always associated it since with polo.

Hong Kong was just as over-populated in those days as it is today, with a torrent of Chinese refugees fleeing from the Japanese war in the north, as well as all the British evacuees arriving from Shanghai. There were, however, one or two places on the island where you could escape from the crowds. My father had been made an *ex officio* member of the famous Sheko Golf Club, where all the taipans took their recreation. It was quite a simple place, although extremely exclusive, and no-one tried to throw their weight about there as they were apt to do in the Hong Kong Club in Victoria.

There was a nice small swimming pool in which even I was quite unable to drown myself, and pleasant cane chairs with cushions for lounging about. Nearby, there was a beautiful bathing beach; and slightly further on still, another beach which hardly anyone went to, called Big Wave Bay. It lived up to its name and there was a dangerous undertow, but we liked to go there because it was usually quite deserted.

Sometimes we went to Repulse Bay, which was a favourite place for all the British families to gather, so we always bumped into friends there. Vera and Elizabeth Black sometimes came with us, to play on the beach with me. We three girls were fascinated by a strange building on the point which stuck out into the bay. It seemed to be made up of endless odd-shaped roof tops and it stretched for several acres along the point. We were told that it belonged to a rich Chinese who had been told by a fortune teller that if he ever stopped building, he would die.

On the other side of the bay was Stanley, which was to become the notorious prison camp for British families, once the Japanese had occupied Hong Kong only a few years later.

On the beach there was a typical 1930's building called "The Lido" where we went for tea. On one occasion, my mother had gone on a trip to Canton with my father, and Miss Gibson and I were taken there by a charming Naval bachelor friend of theirs, who had promised to keep an eye on us during their absence.

I remember that we joined a party of his friends for tea in the Lido. They were very sophisticated people. We did not normally move in those sort of circles, and I was fascinated by the ladies' dark glasses, painted toenails, their dark dresses, and their costume jewellery. The men wore "Noel Coward" scarves round their necks, and beautifully pressed white flannels, and "co-respondents' shoes" in white and brown leather.

They were very noisy and laughed a lot at jokes I could not understand. I gathered that they all went to the races a great deal in Happy Valley and talked a good deal about their winnings.

Suddenly, someone had a bright idea: there was a revolving cake stand in the centre of the table filled with small iced cakes of different colours, a knife was fixed to a teapot as the "winning post", and we each bet on a cake. I was lent my "stake" by our friend. Someone twirled the cake stand and the cake that finally stopped opposite the "winning post" was the winner. I ended up making quite a lot of money, and was regarded with a special sort of attention by my new race-going friends. I suddenly realised that I was a social success, for the first time in my life, and it almost went to my head, until Miss Gibson brought me back to earth again with her disapproving expression.

At weekends, if my father was not away in the *Tarantula,* we used to drive across to mainland China, through Kowloon and on to Fanling, where we kept ponies to ride. Mine was a China pony of about 12 hands called "Leprechaun". Just as I was never to be an expert swimmer, neither did I ever expect to qualify as a confident rider, but I quite enjoyed my rides on Leprechaun, accompanying my father and mother on their slightly larger and more elegant horses. My father's horse was Australian, and my mother's was half-thoroughbred. Leprechaun was elderly and reliable and could be kicked along to lollop over the raised paths between the paddy fields. I never thought he would run away with me, and I never felt as though I might fall off. Best of all, the Chinese grooms always had the ponies ready for us to mount, so there was no chasing after a reluctant pony in a muddy field, while persuading it to be caught with apples, sugar, or buckets of corn. I think I really rather enjoyed riding at that time, knowing that, for once, I did not have to be stable-girl as well.

My parents regularly hunted with the Fanling Drag, and on one memorable occasion I was allowed to take part in a Children's Meet of the hunt. Most unfortunately, Leprechaun had gone lame, so I was put on my father's rather large Australian horse, which must have been about 15 hands and was called "Tula", after his gunboat.

As we streamed off along narrow paths, with flooded paddy fields on either side, "Tula" seemed to realise that I was a novice and I felt she was taking great care of me. I felt vastly superior, especially when I saw a pony in front of me jump into a flooded paddy-field and start swimming around, while the child on its back screamed until rescued by the Huntsman. Then we took to the hills. This was rather different. The trouble there was that the Chinese always bury their ancestors where there is "sanshui" – "hills and water" – both of which abound near Fanling, the scenery being rather like Scotland. Their ancestors' bones are put in large earthenware pots and placed in cavities on the side of the hills, with joss sticks and strange charms made out of coloured glass all round the pot.

Galloping over the hills, following the hounds, it was almost impossible to avoid the hundreds of Chinese "graves". Tula must have been very sure-footed, for I don't remember falling off, though I think I lost my stirrups several times, and frequently had to cling round Tula's neck when the going got rough. I arrived safely at the end of the day, but privately decided I would never go hunting again if I could possibly avoid it. Just as I disliked shooting because of the bangs, so I disliked hunting because of the difficulty of keeping in the saddle. In neither case did I object "on principle". A drag was much more like a paper-chase, so no-one could possibly object to it, and my own real objection was that I thoroughly agreed with the wit who had once commented that the horse is dangerous at both ends and uncomfortable in the middle.

# CHAPTER XIV

D URING THE MONTHS of September and October, while we were sailing out from England in the *Ranchi,* my father had been literally anchored to Canton by the war, and had hardly spent any time in Hong Kong. Fortunately for us, by the end of October, there was a lull in the Japanese offensive, although they continued spasmodically to bomb the railways and aerodromes near Canton.

The Japanese were, however, very anxious to make it clear that the war was entirely limited to China and themselves, so they took great care to avoid bombing areas where the British or the Americans had operations. In Shameen, it was said that a Japanese spy used to let off fireworks during the air-raids to show the Japanese aircraft where *not* to drop their bombs.

They mostly went for the Chinese aerodromes, and eventually prevented any Chinese aircraft from being operated. At the Chinese Naval base at Whampoa, a Chinese cruiser was sunk and also several gunboats. The rest of the gunboats were being hidden away up creeks with trees in their funnels. Chinese defence was reduced to a deplorable state, and there was a woeful shortage of ammunition. Sometimes, when Japanese aircraft flew over Canton on their way north to attack the Hankow Railway flying at around 15,000 feet, there would be a fusillade of pom-poms, machine guns, rifles and even policemen drawing their pistols and firing them into the air. This demonstration was far more dangerous to the local Chinese than to the Japanese planes, who were several thousands of feet out of range.

The ordinary Chinese people took the war totally in their stride, patiently rebuilding their houses and the railways when they were destroyed by bombing, and occasionally removing themselves from Canton to stay with their relations in the country when the bombing got too bad. The only Chinese to panic were the high officials, the governor general, the admiral and their staff, who retreated to dug-outs on the first sound of a warning, changed their offices and houses daily and even tried to take refuge in Shameen, which was the European concession.

The fighting was done by the working class Chinese, who were press-ganged, or joined the army to earn a pittance to avoid starvation. There were very few civilian casualties during the raids, except on one occasion when the Japanese "Formosa" aircraft attacked a parade ground in the town by high bombing, missed it and killed two hundred Chinese in a very poor and crowded part of town. This led to exaggerated reports in British newspapers that Canton had been reduced to rubble, with thousands killed.

Defence in Canton was simplified by the ruthless way in which authorities enforced their orders: if a sampan was on the river at a time when river traffic had been stopped, a police boat would ram it and sink it. Likewise, a coolie walking in the streets during an air raid, or after curfew, would be shot and the body left lying in the street as a warning to others.

The blackout was enforced in the same way, by firing a rifle into a house if a light was shining from it. The air-raid warnings consisted of sirens and, more effectively, police on bicycles and in police boats showing red flags and ringing bells.

My father called on the governor of the province, Wu Te Chen, to convince him that it would be quite impracticable for the Japanese to run destroyers up the Pearl River to attack Canton. Eventually, he managed to persuade him to open the river to ships of a foot draught and below. My father now found his gunboats acting as temporary passenger steamers. On one trip he took fourteen passengers, including a two-week-old Dutch baby and its mother. The river steamers all drew ten or eleven feet, but it was ultimately agreed, by a tacit arrangement, that the river steamers could start to run once more.

By now my father had spent four months in Canton, and was greatly relieved to be able to bring the *Tarantula* back to Hong Kong in time to meet us and to install us at Garden Terrace. Over Christmas and New Year, the *Tarantula* had her annual refit in the dockyard in Hong Kong, so we were able to be together for at least three months before she sailed once more up the West River to Canton, in February 1938.

This time we were able to accompany my father to Canton, though, of course, we did not travel with him in his gunboat but took the river steamer, which had grills round the decks to stop pirates from boarding.

In Canton, the Consul General, called Blunt, most warmly invited us to stay with him. His wife preferred to remain in England, so he lived alone in a huge British Consulate in Shameen and enjoyed having our company. With my predilection for "grand" houses, I was in my element. The house was probably very like some of the houses in Moray Place, or Regent Terrace, in Edinburgh, with high ceilings and classical mouldings. There were also large numbers of Chinese servants to wait on us, and Miss Gibson and I enjoyed ourselves enormously.

We continued with my daily lessons as normal, with one of the many consulate's rooms set aside as our sitting-room-cum-school room.

The air-raids usually took place when there was a full moon, but the people of Canton had got so used to them that one amah, looking after a family of English children in Shameen, had been heard comforting a baby with the words, "Listen to the pretty bomb-bombs, Baby!".

My own feelings about the air-raids were that we must be quite safe with the Union Flag flying over the Consulate. My father never allowed us to call it the Union "Jack" because, he told us, a "jack" was, strictly speaking, only flown from the bow of a ship to indicate her nationality. I did, however, find the air-raid sirens rather alarming and mournful, but soon got used to them. This meant that I had a great advantage over our friends at home, when "our own" war started eighteen months later; air-raids were already something I had experienced with boring regularity.

Because the air-raids at that time never took place in the daytime, so Miss Gibson and I were free to wander the small winding streets amongst the throngs of Chinese, hunting for small "treasures" to add to my collection. I was fascinated, too, by the food shops which sold live chickens, rabbits, lizards, rats, mice and all sorts of delicacies.

My father had eaten Chinese meals on many ceremonial occasions with important Chinese officials. He told us that as long as you did not think about what you might be eating, the food was always delicious. Like most children, I was fairly conservative in my likes and dislikes, but I remember that I particularly enjoyed the way the Chinese prepared their fish in a crisp batter, and I also loved a chicken dish we often had, with bamboo shoots.

I was once given shark's fin soup, which I found quite pleasant, except when you bit on a piece of shark's fin which was like rubbery jelly, the consistency being very nasty indeed, although a great Chinese delicacy. We ate fried rice most days, and I loved the way the Chinese cooked it. Somehow, Europeans never seem to get it to taste the way the Chinese do.

We occasionally used chopsticks, for fun, and I have never forgotten the art. The great advantage of eating with chopsticks in polite society was that you could not put a very large amount into your mouth at one time, so I am sure they were much better for the digestion, and for conversation, than knives and forks. The exceptions were the Chinese we saw eating out of bowls in the streets, who held their bowls close under their chins, shovelling the food in with their chopsticks, which led to loud and satisfying belches.

Spitting was something we soon got used to, as well. All the Chinese did it, all the time, even the grand officials, whose houses were littered with ornamental brass spittoons. We soon realised that spitting was a superstition with the Chinese; it was the only way you could get rid of the devil inside you, they told us.

Walking in Canton, I was lucky enough to see several Chinese weddings, the bride being dressed in red and carried in an ornamental sedan chair, with the curtains closed so that you only got a tiny glimpse of her if you were lucky. I also loved to watch the Chinese jugglers and conjurers who performed in the streets. The best trick of all was the famous one where they sawed a pretty Chinese girl in half. I never did discover how it was done.

Canton was a colourful bustling town, and I enjoyed our expeditions enormously, and felt that *at last* we were in the "real" China – Hong Kong having been far more British than Chinese. Sometimes my parents drove us out into the country, where we saw China as it has been through the centuries, with very little change. The farmers still used hand ploughs, or yoked buffalo, to draw the plough. The rice was planted and harvested by hand, with the whole family taking part; and there were always herds of "walkie ducks" with small boys in charge, and black and white hairy pigs wandering about amongst the smallest children, who always had bare bottoms, which was less bother than wearing nappies.

On the rivers the fishermen used boats made of three strong bamboo poles tied together to make a raft. In our early childhood my father used to sing us a song in pigeon English that he had once been taught, the first line of which was,

"From Foo Chow Foo I come makee walkee,
   three piecy ship, three piecy bamboo!"

I now saw what the song meant. Some of the boats had paddles which were operated like a bicycle, by manpower, so this explained the "come makee walkie" part of the song.

Some of the fishermen used cormorants for fishing, with a ring round their necks to prevent them from swallowing the fish they caught. But this was usually done at night with lamps, so I don't remember ever seeing it.

My memories of Chinese "sanshui" is of distant blue hills and blue water with bright green paddy fields in the foreground. I have always thought that Sanshui was a far better word than "scenery" (meaning, literally, "hills and water"). When I returned to China with my husband forty years later and was lucky enough to be taken to Kweilin (the extraordinary pointed limestone hills being the unique feature, so well known from Chinese art), our young guide, trying out her best English on us, kept telling us that she would show us some more "sceneries". I tried to explain to her that we only used the word in the singular, but she found this totally confusing. "But it must be 'one scenery', and 'two sceneries', is it not?" she insisted. I gave up trying to explain, and once more decided that "sanshui" was far more expressive. The Chinese get most things right, which is why they naturally consider themselves to be vastly superior to the Europeans. After all, they are known as the "Middle Kingdom", between Earth and Heaven, so they are bound to be particularly favoured.

We had arrived in Canton in time for the Chinese New Year, which is in February; and, with my dislike of bangs, I found this celebration distinctly unnerving. Indeed, I think I was far more frightened by the firecrackers that went off without interruption throughout the New Year celebrations, than I was during the air-raids. During the raids the Japanese bombs were always very distant and went off with a dull "thud", unlike the ear-splitting bangs of the Chinese fireworks.

While we were in Canton there was a plot by the Japanese to achieve a "coup d'etat" in the city, and to replace the existing authorities with a pro-Japanese local authority. At this point the Japanese were to bring their ships up the river and land their planes near the city. But they would be unable to bring their army, because the Japanese soldiers were fully deployed in northern China, where they were involved in a difficult and unsuccessful operation.

A heavily-bribed Chinese in Hong Kong who had promised to achieve all this for the Japanese, promptly informed the authorities in Canton of what was intended and sent them the huge amount of money the Japanese had trustingly turned over to him, with which he was supposed to subvert the Chinese troops and officials. As a result, the coup failed and the Japanese airforce were received with vigorous anti-aircraft fire, the most accurate put up by the Chinese gunners to date.

I can remember the noise of the gunfire vividly to this day, but I was still quite convinced that the Consulate's Union Flag was bullet-proof and remember feeling quite unconcerned. The bangs weren't nearly as noisy as the New Year fire-crackers in any case. The air-raids still went on, the worst part of the air-raids being that the electricity and power was turned off at the main switch, to give total enforcement of the blackout. This meant we couldn't use our electric fans and it was beginning to get very hot.

# CHAPTER XV

———— ◆◆◆ ————

I T WAS AT THIS point that I gather my parents began to get concerned about the escalation of the war in China, and decided that, in case it became impossible to get out of the country, it would be wiser to send me back to England. My grandparents had apparently written several times to them to suggest that I should be sent home to Hitcham with Miss Gibson. It was finally decided that she and I should leave by the next P&O ship from Hong Kong.

My father had a job to do, so he had to stay on; although he had now heard that his relief was due to arrive in early June, the job being normally a two-year one. My mother wanted to stay on with him because it would be their first chance to travel home together, and they hoped to do an extensive tour of northern China (the war permitting); and then on through Manchuria, Korea, Japan, to Honolulu, Canada and America – the only time in their lives they would have such a wonderful opportunity to travel together.

I suppose they had always planned to send me home with Miss Gibson in the P&O, so that they could have this wonderful holiday trip together, and I suppose this was probably one of their main reasons for bringing a governess out with us, so that I would have a reliable escort on the voyage home.

But I knew nothing of this, and although I realised I was being sent home because of the war, I also began to think that they did not love me any more and did not want me to stay on with them in China. I was filled with despair. Surely they must know that physical danger was as nothing to being parted from the people you love most in the world? I have continued to believe that children should never be taken away from their parents in dangerous situations. The psychological damage can have a far worse effect on the child, as I believe it did in my case. Even though I was by then nearly ten, I depended greatly on my parents, and I was also far too young to realise that it was quite natural for them to want some time alone together on their own special trip home. I was being sent home because they found me a nuisance, I was convinced, and I cried myself to sleep every night until our ship sailed.

I had always enjoyed scribbling and writing stories, and I wrote rather a moving story at this time, which I have recently unearthed. It told of two little girls who were to be sent to Australia by their parents, from Hong Kong, because of the war. Like me they were distraught. Then a great typhoon blew up one night and the ship they were to travel in was beached in Hong Kong harbour, and they were allowed to stay in Hong Kong after all. I am sure this story was inspired entirely by my own situation; I, too, longed for a typhoon to put the *Rawalpindi* (in which Miss Gibson and I were to sail home) on the rocks.

Unfortunately, nothing like this happened. In fact, the Japanese war started to accelerate to such a pitch that a great many wives and children were already being sent home, although this did not comfort me in the least. I still imagined that I was being "got rid of", and even the generous parting presents our Chinese servants gave me did little to cheer me up.

Now, years later, I value them greatly – a small laughing Buddha with a fat tummy; a little blue horse; a set of tiny white horses, all depicted in various attitudes trying to get rid of an annoying fly (a famous traditional Chinese theme). At the last minute, just when we had everything packed, Ah Tsu arrived with two *huge* glass cases for me, containing beautiful Chinese "fairies" – figures such as one sees in a Chinese opera, complete with flowing robes, ornate head-dresses, and flashing swords.

I almost forgot to be sad when I received Ah Tsu's present – they were the most beautiful things I had ever seen. (Ironically, they were to be destroyed during an air-raid two years later, in our home in the Scottish village of Cardross, in the Second World War.)

Before we left for home, I was given a final treat, and taken on a visit to Macau with my parents. We stayed with a Portuguese family called Gellion, who lived in the first really "modern" house (architecturally) that I had ever seen. It was flat-roofed, with a swimming pool, and everything inside and out was either dazzlingly white, or a cool, pale green. The pale colours that I remember so distinctly were probably decorative Portuguese tiles. I also remember that the dining-room had a mural of banana trees, which was very effective.

I temporarily forgot my misery and much enjoyed seeing this strangely European island, which had kept its Portuguese character since it was first colonised in the sixteenth century, the oldest colony in the Far East.

In the Governor's house there were fine pictures of the famous Portuguese navigators, Gamo, Diaz, Albuquerque and Prince Henry. The churches on the top of the rock were Portuguese and the houses colour-washed, just as they are in Lisbon. The town was spotlessly clean and very prosperous. Its income came entirely from gambling, being the only place in China where gambling was officially allowed. Gambling in China had recently been stopped by the influential Soong family; General Chiang Kai-shek's wife was a Soong and the whole family were Christians, probably originally converted by Scot presbyterian missionaries with "John Knoxian" principles. In fact, "private" gambling continued to be rife throughout China, being in the blood of the Chinese people; but the Soong family had effectively prevented it from contributing to the national income, which would have been far more sensible. In the case of Macau it may have been necessary, for their only harbour was silted up and practically useless, so trading was very limited.

All too soon (and a few days before my tenth birthday), the day arrived when Miss Gibson and I had to board the P&O ship, S.S. *Rawalpindi* to sail home to England. I felt sick with misery, and extremely angry. How could my parents do this to me? In the meantime, my fury was directed at poor Miss Gibson, being the only person handy after we had sailed, and I suspect she must have found me quite intolerable.

Like the pirate twins in my favourite book when we were in South Africa, "I bit my nails, and put out my tongue, and I didn't care". Fortunately for Miss Gibson's equilibrium, I very soon found a real friend. She was called (very suitably as it turned out) Joy. She was the same age as me, and, like me, she used to go riding with her parents at Fanling. We soon found to our delight that there were two rocking horses in the children's playroom and we monopolised them for the whole journey home. The other children never got a look in. The rocking horses were far safer than the real thing as far as I was concerned, and it was the only time in my childhood when I was undoubtedly "pony mad".

I can't think what we pretended to be as we rode those rocking horses day after day, but all I remember was that we were both quite blissful, and Joy was particularly joyous, which cheered me up considerably. I forgot my unhappiness, I forgot Miss Gibson, and I was totally absorbed in the games we played on those two horses. I believe I must have ridden the whole way home from China on mine, during the next six weeks.

Quite soon after the start of the voyage there came a day when we were not allowed to ride the horses. The *Rawalpindi* got caught in the edge of a typhoon in the South China Seas, which was a rare event in a P&O ship. The Japanese were disrupting the weather signals to Chinese shipping at the time and the *Rawalpindi* failed to receive a typhoon warning. For thirty-six hours we were pounded by huge waves and advised to keep in our cabins. I don't remember feeling either seasick or frightened, but thought it was all rather exciting, especially when we heard a great commotion in the corridor outside, and in the next cabin to ours, where there were loud clankings of buckets: two elderly ladies sharing a cabin had decided to have "just a little fresh air, dear," and the whole China Sea had erupted into their cabin through the port hole (or "scuttle" as I had been taught to call it by my father).

It was considered a huge joke by the stewards and stewardesses, luckily, as it was they who had to clear up the mess and mop up all the water. For three days we were forbidden to go on deck because of the huge waves, but Joy and I were allowed back on our horses, so we were perfectly happy.

Then one morning, very early, when the weather was calm again, I stole up on deck as we approached Singapore, before Miss Gibson was awake. I loved being up there alone with only the crew washing the decks and the whole length of the deck to run along as the ship swooped and swung on her course.

Miss Gibson had warned me not to run on the decks when they were wet and slippery; but that day, the first after the storm, I was so glad to be released from the cabin and the playroom into the fresh air, that I tore round the deck pretending I was a bolting horse. Disaster inevitably struck – I slipped on a wet plank and went down on my back, knocking myself out. I remember coming round with stars flashing in front of my eyes and a couple of elderly passengers bending over me asking if I was all right? My first thought was how cross Miss Gibson would be, so I told them I was fine, jumped up and rushed back to my cabin before Miss Gibson got up, pretending nothing had happened.

I must have had a very sore head that day, but I never said a word. Then, the next day I developed a black eye (apparently this can happen after a bang on the head) and the full story had to come out. Miss Gibson was surprisingly kind to me in the circumstances and never said "I told you so", even once.

This episode must have taken place just before my tenth birthday. I was quite convinced that Miss Gibson would forget my birthday and that no-one else on board the *Rawalpindi* would know about it anyway. To have one's birthday ignored is the most terrible thing that can ever happen to a child, and I was in a frenzy of anxiety.

Imagine my surprise when I woke up in my bunk on 20th May, shortly before we arrived in Singapore, to see a pile of presents waiting for me on a chair, and, best of all, a real Chinese doll's pram made of bamboo, from my mother and father, something I had always longed for. In those days, we still played with our dolls at an age when modern girls are probably beginning to be more interested in clothes and boys. The doll's pram was an exact copy of Chinese babies' prams, and I was ecstatic.

Everyone on board the *Rawalpindi* seemed to know it was my birthday and everywhere I went I was greeted with "Happy Birthday!". I couldn't *imagine* how they all knew. At tea the ship's chef had excelled himself, and I had the most beautiful birthday cake I have ever seen, with all the children on board the ship as guests at my totally unexpected birthday party. It was one of the best birthdays of my life and the second of my birthdays to be celebrated on board a passenger ship, my third birthday taking place on the way to South Africa on board the *Dunbar Castle*.

The rest of the voyage home is a sort of blur, probably because I spent most of it on the rocking horses with Joy. I do remember going ashore at Colombo with Miss Gibson, kindly taken by an army wife and her little boy, who were also travelling home; and I remember, too, arriving at Cochin, in south-west India at the mouth of the great muddy river. I went on with my lessons every morning and for the rest of the time I was free to play with Joy. We were inseparable. In Port Sudan we were taken in glass-bottomed boats to see the beautiful coral and brilliantly coloured fishes. The locals had huge frizzy Afro-hair-do's and were known in those days as "Fuzzie-Wuzzies". It was hotter in Port Sudan than anywhere I had ever been.

Suddenly, we were home. And there were my grandparents, with arms outstretched, come to meet us. It was my grandfather who persuaded the customs man to let me bring in a small bonsai tree I had been given. "She's only a little girl, and it is such a little tree!" he said with a persuasive smile. The customs man smiled back and relented.

We were back in England – we were home again. Soon we would be driving through the gates under the old yew trees, and there would be my beloved Hitcham, huge, red, and ugly, but my favourite house in the whole world. As a sailor's daughter I had learnt to avoid putting down roots because of the pain of dragging them up again. But my tap root had gone down deep at Hitcham, because I knew that it was always there to come back to.

# CHAPTER XVI

———————◆———————

**B**ACK AT HITCHAM I soon cheered up. I tore round the gardens to visit the newt in the water-tank and the goldfish in their big circular pond with the tin of dog biscuits and the wooden mallet close by. I broke off a piece of biscuit to crunch and decided it was just as delicious as I had remembered. Near the house the peacocks were proudly displaying their spectacular tails on the front lawn by the copper beech. White fan-tail doves perched on the eaves, waiting for Grandfather to feed them with handfuls of golden yellow corn. In the kennels my friends the labradors, Dusk and Nell, greeted me with soft whines of pleasure. In the stables my eldest uncle's hunters whinnied gently, pushing soft noses towards me to be stroked, hoping that I just might have a lump of sugar on me.

Being the only grandchild at Hitcham, at the time, I had the run of the place, but my favourite rooms in the house both belonged to Grandfather, and because he loved children he let me go into them whenever I wanted. I think he knew how much I was missing my parents, and he offered me his own special sanctuaries to give me the sense of security I so badly needed. He was just the sort of grown-up that children love, quiet with twinkly eyes, small in stature, and with the ability to be companionable without making any demands. I loved him dearly.

Upstairs was Grandfather's dressing-room, lined with huge chests-of-drawers in which all his clothes were kept.

There were no hanging cupboards, because his personal servant always folded his jackets and waistcoats and trousers and laid them in the drawers, after sponging and pressing them. One of the chests had a brushing-tray above the top drawer which you pulled out with two little brass knobs. I liked to watch as his clothes were brushed and sponged – was it by Massey or Bertram? I can't remember. But I do remember curling up in a large arm-chair and chattering happily as I watched. It was very cosy in there.

The other room I liked was Grandfather's study, where I sat as quiet as a mouse while he wrote his letters. It was a tiny room tucked away in the back regions of the house, down a long passage from the hall and through a green baize door. It had very little furniture in it, only a desk and a couple of chairs, and the walls were lined with shelved cupboards for his papers. Everything in the room seemed to be dark brown, but there was nothing gloomy about it, because it had one superb feature which was almost certainly why Grandfather had chosen it as his "holy-of-holies" – a narrow french window opened out into the garden, which meant that he could come and go as he pleased, away from the perpetual stream of visitors invited to Hitcham by Grannie. He called it his "Office", but it was really his escape, and it soon became mine as well. I realise I was enormously honoured.

Grannie was very exciting to be with, because she was full of interesting ideas. But I found her rather unpredictable, even a little overpowering, I was really much happier being with Grandfather. Grannie dressed theatrically in flowing wool or chiffon, with long pointed velvet shoes adorned with silver buckles. I have inherited her long narrow feet, which, unfortunately, means expensive Italian shoes. I expect Grannie's were hand-made. Her beautiful Nordic silver hair was piled on top of her head like a pale shining coronet, giving her the look of a Snow Queen. I have inherited hair that went white at a very early age, just like Grannie's, but as mine has a Celtic curl about it, it would be useless to try to wear it in the elegant style that made my grandmother look so beautiful in old age. Grannie was highly intelligent and a brilliant organiser.

Hitcham, with its large staff and constant flow of family and friends, ran on oiled wheels. Fresh flowers filled all the rooms, and the house always smelled of their scent, mingled with beeswax polish and woodsmoke from log fires. In the winter we had coal fires in our bedrooms, which I remember as a unique form of luxury. Lying in bed looking at flickering shadows from the flames, you could turn them into galloping horses, butterflies, or anything that took your fancy.

Miss Gibson and I carried on with my lessons using the Porch Room, above the front hall, as my temporary schoolroom. In the afternoons we went for walks, or sometimes I went "calling" with Grannie, driven by Berry in the Armstrong Siddeley. This meant visiting the neighbours who lived in impressive houses near Taplow, or beside Burnham Beeches, and leaving "visiting cards". It was a strange social custom of the day, and I know that Grannie and I always prayed that the lady of the house would be "not at home', so that we should not have to sit making polite conversation with a tiny teacup balanced on our knee.

From time to time Grannie had to open a local bazaar, and I went to watch the proceedings, which I found extremely dull. The speeches were always very long and full of compliments to everyone in sight, and I usually ended up yawning and fidgety. It was much more fun feeding the goldfish or making bonfires with Grandfather.

One of Grannie's nicest ideas was to give me another birthday party while I was at Hitcham, to celebrate my recent tenth birthday. I have a photograph to record the event, as we gathered round the rocking horse beside the giant-stride in the garden. Strangely enough, although most of the children Grannie invited were strangers to me at the time, several of them became friends in my later life.

Just after that, I was invited to spend a seaside holiday at Frinton with my youngest cousins, Benny and Juliet. I was just at the age to find small children even more fun to play with than dolls, and I loved helping their Nanny to bath them and dress them, and to dry their toes when they had been paddling. We made huge sandcastles, we ate ice-cream cornets, and we did all the things children love to do at the seaside. Surprisingly, it was the first time I had ever been for a seaside holiday, but then, because I was a sailor's daughter I had lived by the sea nearly all the time, anyway.

While I was at the seaside, Miss Gibson had her first holiday back in Scotland since we had sailed for China. I remember that I travelled by train to Frinton by myself, Grandfather having given the guard a large tip to look after me, and to tell me when to get out. Lots of children travelled like this at a very tender age when I was a child, just in the same way that I now pack grandchildren off on planes by themselves with kind air-hostesses to keep an eye on them.

On my return to Hitcham, Robin arrived from his private school for the summer holidays. I was thrilled to have my brother back with me, and I suddenly realised how much I had been missing him. He was full of silly prep school jokes which made me laugh, and exciting ploys like rowing on the pond, bicycling up and down the huge see-saw, and letting me help him with his Meccano set. We talked a lot to each other, but I have no idea what we talked about. The important thing was that he was my brother, and he seemed very grown up now that he was nearly thirteen. I no longer felt that I had to be completely self-sufficient, as I had done since I left my parents in Hong Kong. My brother was there to look after me now, and he would always know what to do about everything. I had great faith in him. After all, he would soon be going to the Royal Naval College at Dartmouth in a smart uniform, and that made him seem on the threshold of manhood.

I, too, was suddenly becoming more grown up, so much so that I developed mysterious small buttons under my vest, and rushed to ask Robin what they could possibly be. Robin did not look very interested, and said reassuringly that he was sure they would go away again quite soon. They didn't go away, and eventually it dawned on me that my breasts had begun to develop.

It was not long after this that the great day came when my parents arrived home at last. We made huge "Welcome Home" posters and Grandfather hung a large white ensign and a union flag on either side of the front door at Hitcham.

Our little family of four was reunited once more, and I felt secure and happy again. We listened in awe as my mother and father told us all their adventures. They had travelled by land and sea from China by way of Korea and Japan, and then across the Pacific to Canada, with a trip across the Rockies by train, and finally down to New York and home across the Atlantic.

Some of their stories were particularly intriguing: in Japan (because it was known that their journey had started in China, where the war between the two countries was still raging) they soon began to realise that they were being trailed by a sinister little Japanese who even slept outside their hotel bedroom doors at night. Eventually my father decided to ask him if, as he seemed to be attached to them for their trip through Japan, he would mind carrying their suitcases for them? His face crinkled into broad smiles as he bowed and hissed in great delight. Thereafter they became the best of friends, and he proved to be a very efficient porter, in addition to his other more sinister role.

In America they had seen a whole house being transported on the back of a long trailer, they told us. This was how the Americans "moved house" they assured me. It made me wonder if I could make my wish come true and transport our Scottish home, Ardoch, from the Clyde to the shores of Loch Vennachar beside Lendrick Lodge, which was my next favourite house after Hitcham.

The funniest story they told us was about my mother's birthday, which they had celebrated on board the American liner that brought them home across the Atlantic. Apparently the stewards had arranged a surprise birthday cake, and as they carried it in, at dinner, with the candles lit, the band struck up a tune, and everyone suddenly got to their feet. Thinking it must be some sort of national anthem, my father leapt to his feet and stood rigidly to attention. It turned out to be "Happy birthday to you!" and it was the first time they had ever heard what has now become an obligatory part of every birthday party. The idea came from the United States, and it was still quite unknown in England, where, if anyone sang anything, it was more likely to be "For he's a jolly good fellow!"

# CHAPTER XVII

———◆◆◆———

B Y AUGUST 1938, we were back at Ardoch again, this time "en famille" for the first time since we had inherited the little eighteenth century "cottage ornée", or "the neat wee house on the Clyde" as it was originally described by our ancestor, Robert Graham of Gartmore, who had built it. He had designed the house to look like one of the colonial houses he had known when he lived in Jamaica. His wife, Anna, was born in Jamaica, and it reminded him of his happy marriage, before his beloved wife had succumbed to consumption in the cold winds of Scotland, after bearing him five children. He had once written a beautiful love poem to her, starting with the line, "If doughty deeds my lady please, right soon I'll mount my steed". This poem was thought to have been written by his kinsman, Montrose, for many years; but Sir Walter Scott, a close friend of the Grahams of Gartmore, who is reported to have stayed at Gartmore when he was writing *The Lady of the Lake,* found that it had been written by the laird of Gartmore. It later earned its place in the Oxford Book of Verse, and Robert Graham was to be known by his descendants, for posterity, by the nickname "Doughty Deeds". My great-uncle, R. B. Cunninghame Graham, wrote a fascinating biography of his ancestor (called, simply *Doughty Deeds*), and it was probably this man who, as a direct forebear, inspired Uncle Robert more than any other.

Once at Ardoch again, I began to realise that our home on the Clyde did, after all, have a great many delights. There was a huge garden with a lawn that sloped down to the river, a small burn splashing down a miniature ravine with a footbridge across it, a large stable building, and as a finishing touch, my parents has added a hard tennis court, both of them being keen tennis players. That summer we all played tennis almost every day under exceptionally sunny skies. Robin was naturally athletic and was far too good at the game for me, but when we played a foursome I was usually partnered by my mother who had a ferocious underarm serve, which often won us a game. Unlike my brother I was not born with a "ball eye", and on the rare occasions that I managed to return a ball my father used to shout "Baghdad!", and we all fell about laughing, which brought the game to a hilarious close. As a family we never took anything very seriously, so there was always a lot of backchat and laughter whatever we happened to be doing. Croquet was another game that caused us a great deal of mirth, chiefly because our so-called "croquet lawn" was on a slope, so we spent a good deal of time running after the ball as it rolled downhill. The whole thing was reminiscent of *Alice in Wonderland,* which was quite appropriate, being my father's favourite book. He always kept a copy by his bed, with *The Hunting of the Snark,* and could quote long passages from them both, even in his eighties.

At the bottom of our garden there was a railway bridge which led out on to the shore. I loved walking Rogie along the sandy beaches beside the tidal waters of the great river, but it terrified me to have to go under the railway bridge to get there. If a train happened to come over the top when I was under the bridge the noise would "frighten me out of my depth"; it was almost as bad as the heavy guns firing at Simonstown.

The hot weather that summer of 1938 seemed to go on and on, and Robin and I often bathed in the waters of the Clyde, which seemed to be quite unpolluted in those days. (Or was it merely that the word "pollution" had yet to be invented? Perhaps we worried less about those things in the 1930's.) We used to walk through shallow rippling water out to the pools near the deep water channel, where great ships passed by on their way down the Clyde out into the Atlantic. Just as we waved to the engine drivers at the bottom of the garden as they drove their huge steam engines north to Fort William, so we waved to the captains of great ships as they sailed down the river to the "tail of the Bank" at Greenock. As we paddled home again we could see little crabs and purple jellyfish through the clear water, as well as an astonishing assortment of flotsam and jetsam. The most exciting thing we ever found was a bunch of bananas lying on the beach at the high water mark on Christmas Day, 1943. We hadn't seen a banana since the beginning of the war, so it was the best Christmas present we could have wished for!

When the tide went out, the water seemed miles away, and in fact, my father had an old charter which granted our family the right to dredge sand (to sell to builders) "for as far as a man can ride a horse and throw a spear at low tide'; later, I remember one of my small sons (was it Jamie or Sim?) saying excitedly as they looked across the expanse of the tidal water to Port Glasgow, "Look, Mum! I can see a *bus* going along in *America!*" I'm sure it was Jamie, aged three, and he was quite convinced, at that time, that the other side of the Atlantic was just across the Clyde.

The sounds of the Clyde in those days were the dredgers chugging as they kept the deep water channel clear, and the musical notes of hammers on rivets from the many shipyards, few of which are now left. I can hear those familiar sounds to this very day.

At that time the estate of Ardoch had seven farms, and Robin and I got to know the friendly tenant farmers and their families very quickly. They allowed us to bounce on the hay in their barns, and to ride on the bogies when they brought in the "coilies", or ricks. Huge Clydesdale horses pulled the bogies, plodding back to the farmyard from the fields with feathery hooves. Rogie usually managed to find a farm dog with whom to have a satisfying fight during these expeditions.

As well as Rogie, Robin and I were now the proud owners of two ferrets called Roly and Poly. And best of all, I had a pony of my own, which was to live in a field with the highland pony we were to bring back a few weeks later from Lendrick. My mother and I were often to go riding together after that, and I loved to canter along the hard sand on the shore when the tide was out. I was never likely to be "pony mad", but I soon learnt that it was much easier to get to know your pony when you had to look after it yourself.

On 12th August we joined our grandparents, aunts and uncles, and cousins at Lendrick Lodge once more. I was thrilled to be back with "the three musketeers", and this time I also had three much smaller cousins to "mother". Benny and Juliet were there, and my mother's eldest brother had at last got married and produced, not only a delightful new aunt, Esmé, but also, a year later, a baby son. "Little Reg" was still in a pram that year at Lendrick, so I had a real live baby doll to play with. Having been the youngest grandchild until Benny was born, I was now considered to be "one of the older ones", and as such, I seemed to have acquired a new status. One day, "we older ones" decided to write a play and act it for the grown-ups. "Get Jeannie to do it," said Bill, "she's the one who knows about books and things. She's always got her nose in a book. I expect she'll think up a good story for us to act." So I wrote the tale of "The King and the Tinker". It was acted by my older cousins in the drawing-room one night after dinner, and proved to be a tour de force. "Author! Author!" the grown-ups all shouted at the end of the 10-minute performance, and I was dragged forward blushing. I felt I would burst with pride and joy. It was the first time in my life that I had been "a success". "Three cheers for Jeannie!" they called, and my cup was full.

Towards the end of our Lendrick visit everyone seemed to become very tense, and I often heard the words "war with Germany" spoken gravely between the grown-ups. Having recently been in a war in China, and completely untouched by it, I could not think what all the fuss was about. But our parents' faces grew longer and longer, and eventually Grandfather told us that the international situation had become so serious that he had decided to close Lendrick up and return to Hitcham. As a director of the Bank of England and chairman of a big insurance company he realised that he had business responsibilities to which he must urgently return at a time of crisis. This was to be our last holiday at Lendrick. A few days later Chamberlain flew to Germany for his famous conciliatory meeting with Hitler, and the war was temporarily delayed. But the Second World War was only to be a year away.

# CHAPTER XVIII

———◆———

I N MARCH 1939 my father was appointed Captain of the Signal School at Portsmouth. He could hardly believe his luck. He had been offered a rather dull job on his return from China, as a captain on the staff of the admiral commanding Reserves, based in London, which he had turned down.

The important job he had now landed was one entirely after his own heart. He described it as "the best shore job that a captain who had specialised in signals could get". Modestly, he was to add, "No doubt there were no other signalmen captains available'.

This meant another move for us, to a large villa in Southsea called The Red House, in Craneswater Park, which was a pleasant residential area near the boating pond.

In May Robin went to the Royal Naval College at Dartmouth, and was (at his own request) to be called "Robert" from that moment. The Captain of Dartmouth was a friend of my father's called Bob Cunliffe. His daughter Bridget, was to become a great friend of mine, and we both went to the same school, St. Mary's, Calne, in 1941. She now lives in one of England's most historic houses, Knole, in Kent, having married a Sackville West.

I was, at last, sent to a boarding school, but only as a weekly boarder for my first term, slightly to my disgust. It was a very cosy small school near Wickham, only a few miles from Portsmouth, on a pretty estate called Rookesbury Park.

It catered mainly for the children of Naval officers, and to my astonishment and delight I found that my great friend from Hong Kong, Jan Dibley, had fetched up there as well.

My governess, Miss Gibson, left us when I went to Rookesbury Park and I was not to see her again for another forty years, when I was ultimately able to visit her, in her old age, in the little town of St. Boswells in the Scottish Borders. Shortly after that she suffered a severe stroke and was to end her days in a hospital in Kelso. I was deeply touched when her relations brought me a cardboard box, after packing up her cottage, and inside it I found there were all her own Chinese figures, which she had collected when we were in Hong Kong. I felt so sad to think that I probably never appreciated her fondness for me during the years we were together. But I was able to give her a modicum of pleasure, just before her death, when I took my beloved old teddy-bear, Punch, to keep her company in the hospital in Kelso. Her rare shining smile told me all I needed to know.

It was Miss Gibson who grounded me in my education and thanks to her, I found myself near the top of the class at my new school, to my own intense surprise.

Never having been to a proper school before (except a brief term in London at a school in Queen's Gate, called "Miss Ironside's", just before we went to live in Scotland) my new school-friends must have thought me very odd. I was constantly asking them questions about the rules and regulations of the school. I had never lived in any sort of community before, and it all seemed very strange at first. I was allotted a "school mother", a girl the same age as me to show me the ropes; and she rejoiced in the wonderful name of "Petronella Cundy-Cooper". I wonder what has happened to her now?

The hardest part for me was to find myself sharing a large dormitory with at least nine other girls, when I had always in the past slept by myself. (My daughter had exactly the same problem when she first went away to boarding school, but she solved it rather neatly by developing measles very soon after the beginning of term, which meant that she was moved to the Sick Room by herself, to her great joy. She soon found it rather lonely, so was quite glad to get back to her dormitory once she had recovered!)

I was a child who often had nightmares, and sometimes even walked in my sleep. My second night at school I woke up in a panic to find that I had walked into the huge clothes cupboard where all our dresses hung, and I could not find my way out. Fortunately the under-matron must have heard my cries for help, and she came quickly to lead me back to bed with comforting words. I wasn't the least bit unhappy; after all, I had been parted from my parents quite regularly, but I felt very embarrassed that the other girls would think I was an oddity. In fact they were amazingly friendly, and I soon found that I had plenty of real friends, with whom I have kept up for the rest of my life. Petronella Cundy-Cooper was not amongst them, because I think she felt rather superior as my "school mother'.

Two special things about that first term at school remain very vivid: the first was my enrolment as a Girl Guide on a hot summer's day on the front lawn at Rookesbury Park. I was immensely proud of my smart blue uniform, complete with lanyard, whistle, leather belt, and pudding basin hat with its wide brim. From that moment the Girl Guides were to play an important part in my life. As an adult I helped to run a Guide Company, ran a Brownie Pack, was then to be a Brownie Trainer at our Scottish H.Q. After that I became a Commissioner, and Scottish Adviser for handicapped Guides and Brownies ending up as President of the Hawick Local Association; and I once drove four very exalted members of the World Committee from Edinburgh Airport to our Guide Training Centre at Netherurd, in Peeblesshire! But probably my most enjoyable moment as a Guide was when I started up a "Secret Guide Company" at my second school, St. Mary's, Calne, in the walled garden, with sentries posted on the gates, because our headmistress did not approve of Guide Companies at boarding schools. I was fifteen, and I had a band of enormously enthusiastic recruits who enjoyed the whole thing as much as I did, and practised their knots and their Morse code with great diligence! We must have felt rather like the "Early Christians", I suppose.

My second most vivid memory of that first term at Rookesbury Park was the school sports, and the obstacle race in particular. Our headmistress, Miss Glenday, had a clever way of teaching us current affairs, and she wanted us to know all about "The Royal Visit to Canada" which was in progress at the time. It was the first time King George VI and Queen Elizabeth (our Queen Mother, now) had done such an extensive trip abroad, and as Canada was a part of the great British Empire, the tour was considered an important world event, at the time.

Miss Glenday's inspired obstacle race at the school sports mirrored the Canadian Tour of our King and Queen, and we had to negotiate all sorts of hazards such as "Icebergs in the Atlantic", "Grizzly bears in the Rocky Mountains", as well as, amongst other things, performing special tasks as "Red Indians" and "Mounties". It was the best geography lesson I have ever had!

I remember feeling rather sorry for Princess Elizabeth and Princess Margaret Rose who had been left behind at Windsor, not far from Hitcham, where I had spent the previous summer also separated from my parents. Princess Elizabeth was two years older than me and Princess Margaret Rose a year younger than me, so I could identify very closely with them. (My other childhood heroine was Shirley Temple! She was exactly the same age as me.)

We were back at Ardoch for the summer holidays, but there was to be no Lendrick that year. Everyone was talking once more about the threat of war, and it seemed that Hitler was not to be a man of his word. During the crisis we had seen trenches being dug in Hyde Park, and buildings being sandbagged. But then we all fell into a state of false security for several more months. Now it was beginning to look as though it was to be "for real" again. On 1st September Hitler invaded Poland with his troops, and on 3rd September war was declared.

We had Bill and John spending their holidays with us. They were both at Winchester by now, and the "three musketeers" were feeling very self-important now that two of them were public-schoolboys and the third a Naval cadet. But we still had the same jokes and fun, the special activity of the holidays at Ardoch being to make a tree-house at the top of the large weeping ash by the orchard.

It was Bill's fourteenth birthday on the day War was declared, 3rd September 1939, and there was a colossal thunderstorm in the afternoon, during which the rain came down in torrents and water poured down the grassy slope behind the house flooding our kitchen. So that is my chief memory of the first day of the Second World War, cleaning up the kitchen with mops and buckets, and rescuing packets of sausages and biscuits floating round in the flood. Eventually we got round to eating Bill's birthday cake, and realising suddenly, that we were "at War".

It was later that evening that I saw my mother in tears on the telephone to my father, who was stuck in Portsmouth. After she had put the receiver down I rather naïvely asked her why everyone was so upset by the news. The war in China hadn't seemed so terrible to me, and I suppose I was too young at eleven to realise how protected from it we had been, living in the British Legation on Shameen Island in Canton.

I remember my mother's answer to my question very clearly, "You see, darling," she said, "the really awful thing will be if the Germans use *gas*. It was quite frightful what it did to people in the last war. That's why you MUST take your gas mask with you absolutely *everywhere*, darling."

She was very self-controlled by then, but she must have been worried sick being parted from my father at such a grave moment. No-one knew, that day, when the Germans would drop their first bombs, and we all expected the air-raid sirens to go off at any minute. We had been issued with our gas-masks a few days before, and, with the innocence of childhood we thought them hilariously funny. We made grunting noises like pigs, and bounced out at each other from behind doors wearing them, to give each other a fright. I can remember their rubbery smell to this day, just as I can remember the feel of the cardboard box container bumping on my bottom as it swung from a piece of string over my shoulder.

The possibility of the Germans using gas on civilians in Britain, in 1939, was as frightening to us as the idea of the atom bomb was to be to the post-war generation. In both cases, thankfully, our fears proved to be groundless. Even the scientists who had developed the atom bomb had severely frightened themselves by the end of the War after seeing the devastation and human agony in Japan, caused by the first atom bomb.

Perhaps the dreadful effects of gas on the soldiers of the First World War made the Germans think again, too, about using it in the Second World War. Fortunately for us we never had to wear our gas-masks in a gas attack, and we continued to think of them as objects of amusement, or just a plain nuisance. Perhaps the best joke of all was the one we all read in the leaflet supplied with our gas-masks, which told us, in the event of a gas attack, to "put your hands in your coat pockets, and *then* to put up your umbrella". And they were quite serious, apparently!

# CHAPTER XIX

D URING THE SUMMER holidays of 1939 my school
evacuated to South Devon, so I got my wish, the next
term, and became a full boarder. We were now
installed in a stately pile near Newton Abbot, called Haccombe
House, and we found it decidedly bleak and unfriendly. Not
unnaturally, the owners had removed anything remotely
valuable, like carpets and pictures, so we had linoleum on the
floors, desks in the classrooms, and iron bedsteads with lumpy
mattresses in the dormitories. If we dared to complain, someone
was sure to say, "Don't you know there's a war on?"

My parents were greatly relieved to know that Robert and
I were in comparative safety in Devonshire, and it was
convenient for them to be able to visit us simultaneously, on the
rare occasions when they were able to come and see us, which
was never more than once a term. I was always to find saying
goodbye extremely painful, so I believe I honestly found it a
relief to know that school was school, and home was home, and
that "never the twain shall meet". I could cope perfectly well
with my two different lives, but when they touched, my
fortitude fell apart. It is always embarrassing to a child to have
their parents wandering round their school, for one thing, they
don't know the rules and it is quite likely that they will make a
loud remark in a passage where "we are never allowed to talk,
because we are passing the Headmistress's study". It never

occurs to the child that their mother and father might be immune from school rules, because they are actually paying the fees. We all lived in terror of our parents making some frightful *faux pas* when they came to take us out, and this dimmed the pleasure of seeing them. Their letters, on the other hand, were our greatest joy; how happy a familiar hand-writing on an envelope can make you, when you are parted from loved ones. The telephone has never come remotely near that delight for me. After all, a letter can be read over and over again, when you are away from home.

It was the isolation of Haccombe House that I hated most of all. The huge park circled us in its arms, so that we never heard a car going past, nor saw a stranger walking by. It was totally claustrophobic, but I never thought of running away. I believe that Miss Glenday did everything in her power to try to make this daunting mausoleum into a sort of a home for us all. Her own room had been the drawing-room of the house, and it was the one room with character. It had beautiful furniture and a soft blue carpet, and every evening Miss Glenday used to read the whole school a bedtime story as we curled up on the floor around her armchair. It was the one moment in the day when I felt happy.

By the summer of 1940 we knew that we were in danger of being invaded by the Germans. Each of us had a small packed overnight case under our beds for such an emergency, we wore identity discs, and our gas-masks in their cardboard carrying boxes sat on our bedside chairs. We could hear the bombers flying over, night after night, and we began to recognise the German planes by the strange syncopated thrumming noise they made.

We children had to be prepared for any eventuality, just like the grown-ups. Miss Glenday had let us listen to Mr Churchill's rousing words on her wireless, and I really believe that we, too, were ready to defend "the beaches" (we had come to know some of them when we went for school picnics to the small coves that were within walking distance of Haccombe House).

One night I woke up suddenly to hear the sound of armoured cars approaching Haccombe House up the long drive through the park. No cars ever came up our drive except the milkman and the postman, and certainly never at four in the morning. I lay rigid with terror as the vehicles rumbled into the cobbled courtyard at the back of the house. Should I wake up the rest of the dormitory? It was obvious that the Germans had invaded. And then I heard a blessed English voice, swearing an extremely rude Anglo-Saxon oath. It transpired that they were our own soldiers who had got lost on a night exercise! I have often thought, since, that I must be the only person in the whole British Isles who actually thought, one night in 1940, that the Germans really had landed on our shores. I have never had a more anxious moment.

Shortly after that, my mother took me out from school and gave me lunch in the Grand Hotel in Torquay. The first reports of Dunkirk were coming through, and we heard over the wireless, in the main lounge of the hotel, of the armada of brave little boats that had set out across the Channel to bring back our beleaguered army. Many of them came from small seaside towns near my school on the south coast of Devon, and almost everyone in Torquay knew of some yachtsman or fisherman who had gone to the rescue with his boat, regardless of the awful danger. My mother did not realise at the time that her own youngest brother was reported missing, but to our great relief he turned up a few days later, safe and sound. (This was the father of Benny and Juliet.) After she had taken me back to Haccombe House, my mother went to catch her own train back to Portsmouth from the station in Newton Abbot. As she was waiting for her train, the first troop-trains started to arrive, crammed with exhausted soldiers, and she joined the many other passengers who bought up the contents of the station buffet to distribute to the hungry and thirsty men. The safe evacuation of so many men was considered to be a miracle, especially as the weather stayed fine throughout. Gales in the Channel would have meant disaster for the hundreds of "cockle-shells" which so bravely crossed to Dunkirk that day, to rescue the British Army.

Meanwhile, Portsmouth was receiving the nasty end of the "Battle of Britain", as bombs rained down every night. Often my mother and father were at different ends of the town during the raids, wondering if each other was still alive.

My father was involved in the development of radar at the time, known in those days as "R.D.F.'; and also in experiments with infra-red signalling, which was only visible to the recipient. The Signal School was also trying out television, for reporting the enemy from aircraft. Naturally all these new ideas were top secret, and we had not the slightest idea of what went on in the Signal School. A great many top civilian scientists and experts had been co-opted by the Navy for this work, and my father found himself surrounded by some of the cleverest men in the country. They were all very short of sleep, because of the constant bombing night after night. However, a visit to the Signal School by King George VI raised their morale enormously, and my father enjoyed reminiscing with the King about happy times at Balmoral when they were boys. Because my grandfather, Commander Charlie Cunninghame Graham, had been a "Groom-in-waiting" to King George V, it meant that he always went to Balmoral when the King was there; and my father, as a boy, used to shoot and fish with the two princes, David and Bertie, being the same age. The house they were lent was called the Mains of Abergeldie, quite close to Balmoral Castle.

While my father was busy trying to get the fleet equipped with the newest technology as quickly as possible, my mother was fully occupied working in an empty house (commandeered by the head of the W.R.N.S., Mrs Laughton Matthews) sorting references of would-be W.R.N.S. recruits. By asking for three references for each girl it was much harder to get into the "Wrens" than the other two women's services, and human nature being what it is, this made it the most popular service to join. My father was using "Wrens" a great deal at the Signal School, because it had been proved that they made quicker wireless operators than men, so they were much in demand.

My mother managed to get away to take Robert and me to Ardoch for the school holidays. I remember the Christmas holidays in 1940. The Lake of Menteith, near Gartmore (from where our family originally came) froze over, and we managed to save up enough of our petrol ration to drive there from Ardoch for a wonderful day's skating. Bill was staying with us again, so there were enough of us to have a make-shift game of ice hockey, which we played with walking sticks, fast and furiously – I shall never forget the huge expanse of shining ice between the Port of Menteith and the Island of Inchmahome; it was like skating on icing sugar, and we went like the wind.

The Clyde Blitz, when the Germans vigorously attacked the shipyards night after night, began unexpectedly during our Easter holidays in 1941. Our first evacuees arrived to stay at Ardoch then, bombed out of their "single end" in Clydebank. The two Taylor girls and their young brother seemed relatively unaffected by their traumatic experience, but their mother was a bundle of nerves. Each time the air-raid siren went off she would start to shake, and we had to calm her with frequent cups of tea during the subsequent raids.

Then it was *our* turn; and, on a night when high-explosive bombs rained down on the nearby village of Cardross, completely destroying our parish church, a lone plane decided to jettison its bombs, before making for home, and they landed within forty to fifty yards of our house.

Having sat up, night after night, during the raids, we were all feeling terribly tired, so once the anti-aircraft guns had fallen silent, and the last wave of German planes appeared to have finished their devilish work, my mother suggested we should all go to bed. The mistake we made was to ignore A.R.P. warnings that everyone must, if at all possible, take shelter until the "All Clear" sounded. That night, because the raid seemed to be over at last, we all trooped off to bed; but the "All Clear" had *not* in fact been sounded.

It was then that the most extraordinary thing of my whole life happened to me: being rather unnerved by the frightening raid I asked my mother if I could spend the rest of the night in her bed with her. It was the only occasion that I can remember asking such a thing, and I was, after all, nearly twelve-years-old. My own bedroom was next to Robert's on the ground floor (Ardoch having been originally built as a colonial "bungalow'), but in Victorian times a little "turret" was built above, in which was my parents' bedroom and bathroom, up a steep staircase.

We settled down comfortably in her big bed, and then I heard a single plane approaching. It came closer and closer, and it seemed to be flying unnaturally low. Perhaps it had been hit? Then came the terrifying screaming sound of a stick of bombs falling on our house, followed by the appalling crashing of masonry and shattered glass , a sound like the end of the world. My mother pulled me down under the thick quilt and we clung together while the terrible noise of destruction went on and on.

Suddenly it became unbelievably quiet, and my mother leapt out of bed with one distraught word, "Robert!" Her first thought had been for the child who was in another part of the house; had his bedroom been smashed? We raced down the steep staircase which was covered with broken glass from a skylight (why we did not cut our feet to ribbons I shall never know) and rushed through the house to Robert's room, just as a tousled head came round the door with the sleepy inquiry, "What on earth was that? It woke me up." He sounded so indignant that we burst out laughing with relief. Soon the evacuee family appeared, too, with our cook, Sarah. They were all safe.

Then we went to look into my bedroom, and the most appalling sight met our eyes: the ceiling had collapsed on my bed, all my Chinese "treasures" were smashed, and huge jagged pieces of glass were embedded in the walls, the floorboards, and the furniture. My mother held me very tight to her, gasping "Oh my darling, *thank God* you weren't in your own bed. You must have a very special guardian angel." And that is what I have thought ever since.

# CHAPTER XX

——◆◆◆——

WHEN MY FATHER got our telegram to say that all the windows at Ardoch had been blown out and there were several ceilings down, he managed to rush to Scotland for a few days' leave. He could hardly believe that, having sent us away from Portsmouth to the *safety* of Scotland, we had landed straight into the Clyde Blitz. It was ironic, to say the least.

Robert and I soon left for the summer term, travelling south by night sleeper, as we always did, and having breakfast in London with my Aunt Olave (my father's elder sister), before catching our school trains. There was an air-raid taking place in London as our train from Glasgow approached Euston Station, so it was stopped until the All Clear had sounded. We could hear muffled thumps in the distance, but since "our bomb" at Ardoch, very little could frighten us, and we scanned the skies hopefully for "dogfights". The barrage balloons looked golden and beautiful as the sun rose. We had caught the spirit of the dogged Londoners, since we had been a part of the Clyde Blitz. The Germans were never going to win, whatever they did to us.

At the end of my final term at Haccombe House we had "The Great Rat Scandal". It all started when we began to keep silkworms in shoe-boxes in our lockers. There was a beautiful old mulberry tree on the lawn, and silkworms eat mulberry leaves. So silkworms became the new craze. Before long they had woven the most gorgeous gold silk cocoons. Shortly after that the cocoons started to disappear, and nobody could think where they had gone to, or who could possibly have taken them. Then one of the small girls came running to tell Miss Glenday that she had found the most beautiful golden nest behind the radiator, and it was full of baby rats! The whole thing was beginning to get more like St. Trinians every day, and there was worse to come: we had often heard strange scuffling sounds in the long passages outside our dormitories at night, and now it transpired that there was a plague of rats at Haccombe House. On the last night of term I went to bed with my luggage packed beside my bed for an early start by train next morning, in company with the rest of the school, when suddenly a rat shot into our dormitory and settled down for the night under my bed. I hardly slept a wink all night, as I kept hearing it moving about under my bed. Early next morning the young matron came in to wake us up, and I said, "Please Miss Gray, but there's a rat under my bed."

"Nonsense!" she said, peering under the iron bedstead. At that moment the rat rushed out, and with great presence of mind, she seized my hockey stick and felled it with a swipe. We all felt rather sick as she removed it by its tail. I was distinctly relieved to be leaving Haccombe House for good, although I gather that the "rodent operator" cleared the house of rats before the next term began. That was my very last night at Haccombe House.

To my great joy we were going to spend the summer holidays at Yelverton, quite near to Plymouth. The bombing was still continuous on the Clyde, so we could not go to Ardoch. Also, my father had just been appointed Captain of H.M.S. *Kent,* a battle-cruiser of 14,000 tons, of the County Class, so he would soon be going to sea again. For the time being, the ship was being refitted at Devonport. Best of all, Jan Dibley's father was Engineer-Rear-Admiral of Devonport Dockyard, so, once again, we would be able to spend some time together during the holidays. But we had not counted on the Germans, and now we were to witness the sad bombing of

Plymouth, though fortunately we were too far from the town to suffer any damage ourselves. Wherever we went a new blitz started, and we began to wonder if it was our fault!

I can well remember the strange sight of Mutley Plain, in Plymouth, where some of the best shops had been. It was now reduced to rubble. Jan and I rode our bicycles through the ruins (the bombing raids only happened at night, so we did perfectly ordinary things in the daytime), and I gave myself a fright when my bicycle wheel got caught in a tram-rail, and I nearly went over the handle-bars.

Jan and I bicycled a lot together during those "hols", and one glorious day we were allowed to take a small train from Yelverton to Princeton on Dartmoor, so that we could ride all the way back on our bikes. We were very intrigued to see the prisoners from the famous Dartmoor Prison, hoeing vegetables in the fields under the sharp eye of warders. The prison itself looked very gloomy and sinister.

Every child in Yelverton rode a pony, and I was no exception. I even took part in a gymkhana for the first time in my life. Most mornings I went riding with my parents and Robert before breakfast, and I shall never forget the beauty of Dartmoor with its heather and golden bracken, and wild ponies wandering through the small stunted trees. We seemed to be very far from the horrors of war when we went riding together.

Jan and I were both going to the same new school the following term, it was St. Mary's, at Calne, in Wiltshire. The education was supposed to be very good, and the headmistress, Miss Matthews, an outstanding example of one of the pioneering women who did so much for girls' education in the first half of the twentieth century.

H.M.S. *Kent* was shortly to sail to Scapa Flow, having been fully repaired after suffering the indignity of a hit by an Italian torpedo off the North Africa coast, as well as some damage from a near miss in Devonport Dockyard during the recent blitz. We watched her sail, in company with all the wives and sweethearts of the ship's company, and we all secretly wondered when we should see our loved ones again. My mother was always very brave about partings, as sailor's wives have to be, but I could tell how gulpy she was feeling. She was going back to Ardoch as soon as she had seen me off to my new school.

Fa (as we always called him) admitted to us later that he had been extremely nervous, though preserving an appearance of calm, about getting the *Kent* to her first buoy. He described it as a memorable adventure to be taking his new large ship out to sea for the first time, and he was highly relieved to find that he had a navigator, Charles Cree, who had a natural gift for ship handling. His commander, George Oswald, was a gunnery specialist, and was to become one of my favourite people. (His son, Julian, has just, as I write these words, retired from being the First Sea Lord, fifty years later. How proud his father would have been.)

Once at sea, my father was particularly interested to see the performance of the ship's R.D.F. (radar) which he had been in charge of developing while captain of the Signal School.

I had been on board the *Kent* before my father sailed, and had been shown round the ship by a shy midshipman. He must have been rather fed up to be told to take the captain's thirteen-year-old daughter on a tour of the ship – "Show her everything!" my father had told him cheerfully – but he proved to be a most interesting guide, and he certainly showed me everything. When we arrived back in my father's cabin I said excitedly, "We've seen absolutely *everything,* even the R.D.F.!" There was an awful silence, the midshipman went bright red, and Fa looked unchacteristically severe. "That was the one thing you *weren't* meant to be shown," he said quietly. Nevertheless, he invited the midshipman to join us for tea, and nothing more was said. I only hoped the poor midshipman wasn't going to have his leave stopped.

R.D.F. was still top secret and very experimental. Apparently when the *Kent* reached the Clyde Estuary on her cruise to Scapa Flow, the new radar failed to reveal a large convoy with its ships darkened and almost invisible. It was an alarming encounter, and they only sighted the convoy just in time to reduce speed and avoid running into the middle of it at 22 knots.

For the next two years the *Kent* was to hunt out U-boats as she patrolled the two passages between Iceland and the Orkneys and Shetlands (the Black Patrol), and between Iceland and the pack ice edge off Greenland (the White Patrol). The weather could be equally savage in both, though the Denmark Strait (White) could be colder. In the low twenties the frozen spray turned the *Kent* into a sort of wedding cake. There would be literally hundreds of tons of ice coating the ship, which was dangerous for trawlers and small craft, but did not affect so large a ship as the *Kent*.

I was later to discover that my future father-in-law, Charles's father, Captain Jack Jauncey, was involved in the same area, as captain of the *Palomares*, an anti-aircraft ship, escorting the tragic PQ17 convoy. His brave actions that day earned him a D.S.O. He was an outstandingly delightful person, and I only wish he had lived to see his seven Jauncey great-grandchildren, to whom I have dedicated this book.

The *Kent* was also to escort convoys to Murmansk and back three or four times, and on one occasion they took the Foreign Secretary, Anthony Eden there and back. It was on that trip that news came through that Pearl Harbour had been attacked by the Japanese and that America was now in the war with us. My father had the unusual duty of informing the Foreign Secretary of this vitally important signal. The ship was sent to Liverpool for her refit after this trip, at Cammell Laird's yard, and we joined my father for part of our holidays, staying at Hoylake. Once again there was a blitz on Liverpool while we were there; it always seemed to happen, everywhere we went!

Meanwhile, I had arrived at my new school with Jan, and we both thought it a huge improvement on Haccombe House. Jan's father had been moved to the Admiralty in Bath, where they now had a house, so I stayed with them the night before we went to St. Mary's, and Jan's parents took us to see Donald

Wolfit acting in "Hamlet". It was the first time I had been to a Shakespeare play, and I thought Donald Wolfit was exactly how I had imagined Hamlet to be; it was one of the best productions I have ever seen – or perhaps everyone feels that, the first time they see a Shakespeare play on the stage, instead of as a subject for a school exam.

Settling into my new school was very easy, as several of my special friends from Rookesbury Park and Haccombe House were there too. Our fathers were all in the Navy, and we were teased by the other girls for forming an exclusive "Naval clique". But that was not really the case at all, because St. Mary's was a particularly friendly school, and I soon had new friends whose fathers did all sorts of interesting things. A good many of them were in the armed forces, because of the war, but there was also a good sprinkling of clergymen (the school had originally been founded for the daughters of the Anglican clergy) and also farmers, university professors, doctors, lawyers, and all the other professions.

I was always to feel, while I was at St. Mary's, that we were under the powerful influence for good of our much loved headmistress, Miss Matthews, or "Matt" as we all called her. She treated us as individuals and helped to develop our potential while we were in her care, which is the most important thing any headmistress can achieve. She managed to give us a tremendously strong but natural faith, and she cleverly instituted a competition in which we had to learn by heart large chunks of the Bible and the Book of Common Prayer, equipping us with a most valuable resource for life. When we had learnt the whole lot, we were tested, and if we were word-perfect we won our "Lilies", the school crest (madonna lilies) engraved on a special book marker. I have mine to this day.

Matt was considered to be quite a "character", and we often had glimpses of her eccentricities. On one occasion she was shepherding the school across the Bath Road in a long crocodile to go to church on Sunday, when she found our way blocked by an interminable army convoy. Eventually decided we were all going to be late for church, so she strode

170

out in front of the tanks and armoured cars, holding up her umbrella. The convoy came to a halt and a furious young officer came up on a motor bike to see what the hold-up could be.

"I have to get my girls to church," said Matt quite calmly.

"Don't you know there's a war on?" blustered the young officer. But Matt was busy hustling us across the road and did not seem to hear.

The school had grown very quickly in recent years, so some of us slept in houses in other parts of the town. My favourite one was St. Bridget's which overlooked the town square. I loved feeling that I was part of the "real world", and not cut off like we had been at Haccombe House. To get to St. Bridget's we had to go along a tiny lane with high walls on either side, called The Slicket. I suspect it was Calne's "lovers lane", and we often had to pass embracing couples hidden in dark corners. But in those days there never seemed to be much local "crime", and we were considered to be perfectly safe walking by ourselves down the Slicket to St. Bridget's. The grown-ups were much more worried that we might be run over by a car in the black-out, so they hit on a clever idea, which was to get us to sew wide bands of white linen, from old sheets, round our pale blue school cloaks. We could have been seen a mile away!

We all worked very hard at our lessons at St. Mary's, which meant that exams held few fears for us, and Matt used to boast that her girls *always* passed their School Certificate before they left. To make quite sure, she would tell us that *if* the whole *form* passed, then the *school* could have a whole holiday. After that, we simply had to, or we should have let the whole school down! But Matt gave us unexpected holidays for other things too: if an Allied victory was announced we always had a whole holiday, and likewise, if the father of one of the girls was given a decoration for bravery we had a whole holiday for that, too.

Once, Matt decided to cheer us up during a patch of very gloomy weather, so she announced a whole holiday, and we could each collect our picnic lunch in a paper bag, and eat it anywhere in the school that appealed to us! Somehow, she managed to make life fun for us all, which was something my father wholeheartedly approved of, having much the same ideas for running a ship.

Matt also managed to get us to absorb a great deal of unusual information. At the end of every term we had a test on the dates of the Kings and Queens of England ("Willy,Willy, Harry, Ste ... " etc. etc.); and in the summer term we were tested on the names of all the roses and the herbaceous flowers in the walled garden. Every year on Ascension Day we had to do a very difficult General Knowledge paper, after which we went for a glorious picnic amongst the azaleas in the grounds of Bowood, by kind permission of Lord Lansdowne.

Another of Matt's good ideas was to make sure that we all had a really quiet Sunday once a month, so we had what we called "Long Rest", when we all had to retire to our houses for the afternoon to lie on our beds, with our books and our weekly sweet ration, which we were given on Sundays. This was my idea of absolute bliss, and I think it still is, to this day!

Once we had taken our School Certificate, Matt would urge us to stay on for a further "examless" year at school; during which, thanks to her many local contacts, she would give us the chance to try out the career we hoped to pursue when we left school. As I wanted to teach, she arranged for me to go once a week to a small country primary school within bicycling distance, which I thoroughly enjoyed. I had hoped to go on to Oxford University, but it turned out that, even though I had obtained "exemption from matriculation" with my School Certificate results, there would be very few places for schoolgirls during the coming year, because they were rightly being offered to girls who had served in the war. But Matt told me that I would do just as well to go to the Froebel Educational Institute at Roehampton, run by her great friend, Miss Eglantyne Jebb (who was later to be the founder of "Save the Children') and there I would not only be trained as a teacher, but I should also be able to take three advanced subjects for my own benefit, which would give me a far broader base than a university degree. I was always to be grateful to Matt for this excellent advice, which has helped to give me such a full life. If the war had still been going on when I left school, my first intention was to join the "Wrens", but that was not to be.

During that final year at St. Mary's I was lucky enough to be taught European history by Matt, who made it all come alive in an inspired manner, giving us some good laughs at the same time. She used to tell us that she was related to the famous Dr Spooner, and she did indeed have trouble with words, just like him. The best one of all was when she was teaching us about the Napoleonic Wars, and as she got more and more excited, describing a sea battle, we were enchanted to hear her say,

"And then, the flannel sheet rushed to the rescue!"

Matt was very keen on crash courses, but in her case she planned them not just for an individual or for a class, but for the whole school. And so we had Greek Week, and French Week, and the most inspired and progressive one of them all, "Town and Country Planning Week", when we learnt all about the new motorways that would be built after the war with their "clover-leaf crossings", and about huge enterprises like the Tennessee Valley Authority in the United States. Matt was, indeed, very far in advance of her times, and she always seemed to know the right expert to come and tell us about these things. She was a very remarkable woman, with the broadest possible outlook.

I have left to the last the many musical activities at St. Mary's. Another expert was found by Matt for our musical inspiration, in the person of the great Reginald Jacques of the Bach Choir. He became our Director of Music, and in due course he invited us to take part in the Bach Choir's "St. Matthew Passion" in the Albert Hall. We were enormously excited to be going to London, but to our intense dismay, Adolph Hitler frustrated the whole plan by sending over his "Doodle Bugs", the flying bombs, and Matt knew that she could not risk sending us to London under the circumstances. We were bitterly disappointed. But we still had plenty of music, with our school orchestra and choir, our individual instrumental lessons, and even a "school ballet" danced to music by Chopin.

I have left out the names of the many teachers who taught us our lessons under Matt's leadership, but, just like a "happy ship" in the Royal Navy, so we had the benefit of a happy staff. Of course there were the ones we hated, and the ones we liked, and of course we made up silly jokes, like the one that went, "The staff of life is bread, and the life of the staff is one long loaf!" which we thought was hilariously funny. Matt very sadly died only a year after she retired, and in an obituary by Doreen Urwick, she says about her, "Born in another age perhaps Miss Matthews would have been the Abbess of some great foundation, keeping alive the spiritual heritage of the Middle Ages in a more worldly way; building in stone, enforcing discipline, and yet always with time to speak to one homesick or naughty novice."

During my last term at St. Mary's two of my contemporaries pretended to be two young mothers coming to look over the school for their daughters. They were brilliantly disguised, and they thought they had carried the whole escapade off without being recognised by Matt, as she showed them round the school in all seriousness. At our prize-giving, on the last day of term, Matt announced that she had a special prize for two very talented young actresses; imagine their surprise when the two "tricksters" realised that they were the prize winners!

Matt loved any sort of enterprise or initiative, and was always prepared to join in the laughter at any joke against herself. She was an inspiration to us all, and how proud she would have felt is she could have known that St. Mary's, Calne, was to come eleventh out of the top 500 schools in a table printed by *The Times* on 7th September 1993.

# CHAPTER XXI

B Y 1943 MY father had, to our great relief, handed over
H.M.S. *Kent* to Captain Geoffrey Hawkins, married to
one of two sisters who were the daughters of the Duke
of Buccleuch, and who both married sailors. (The other married
Peter Dawnay.) Anne Hawkins, his daughter, was to become
one of my own great friends, and I was proud when I heard that
she had become Assistant Press Secretary to the Queen in due
course, and was later made a D.C.V.O. We had a very special
link, because our two fathers had both been captains of H.M.S.
*Kent;* the ship another of her captains, Bertie Packer, used to
call "The Fair Maid of Kent". His South African wife, Joy, was
later to write her memoirs of the war years, calling the book *The
Grey Mistress,* which was her own name for the *Kent.* She knew
very well that her greatest rival as the wife of a sailor was his
*ship*.

My father's new job was to be Commodore of Chatham
Barracks, where he was to be in command of 24,000 officers,
men and women, with a turnover of 1,000 a day – some 500
coming into the barracks, and 500 going out. He used to say that
he probably had the job of two army divisional generals, but
with far fewer attendant high-ranking subordinates.

At the beginning of the war the numbers in the Royal
Navy were around 110,000. By the end of 1945 they had risen
to 750,000.

We now had yet another house, and this time it was an "official" one. The Commodore's House in Chatham Barracks was large and comfortable, and we had a full staff of charming Naval stewards, to my mother's great delight. We also had a great deal of entertaining to do, from visiting V.I.P.'s, to the children of my parents' friends who had joined the Wrens, or become Able Seamen. One of these Wrens was another of the Buccleuch family, the Duke's daughter, Elizabeth, who was to become Duchess of Northumberland. She was a great favourite of ours, and I am told that she led the Chatham Wrens into all sorts of pranks with her high spirits.

After spending my school holidays quietly at Ardoch (apart from our one stay at Liverpool) for the two years that my father had spent at sea, it was very exciting at the age of fifteen to find myself at the hub of a huge Naval establishment.

It was the climax of my childhood as a sailor's daughter. I was immensely proud when I saw my father taking the salute at Sunday Divisions, and I loved to go to church with my parents in the Barracks Church, listening to the deep musical voices of the sailors as they sang "Eternal Father strong to save, whose arm doth bind the restless wave".

D-Day was approaching, and there was much to-ing and fro-ing in our house, with captains and admirals hurrying in and out. Sometimes my father would have to take a very hush-hush telephone call in our drawing-room, and we took the hint when he smiled at us and said "Crumbs in your ears!" which meant that we mustn't listen. But my father was to tell us afterwards that even he had no idea what date D-Day was going to be, the invasion of Europe by the Allies. On the great day itself, at St. Mary's, we watched wave upon wave of huge gliders flying over the school, and we knew that the invasion of Europe had begun. It was a strangely exhilarating day.

Robert was now at sea, and in due course he came home on leave with a brand new gold stripe on his sleeve as a newly fledged sub-lieutenant. Hitler's "doodle-bugs" flew interminably over us at Chatham and we soon got used to them, although we still held our breath if the engine cut out, knowing that there would be an immediate explosion. One day I went with a friend to see *Gone With the Wind* in the local cinema, and when we came out all the buildings on the other side of the road had been demolished by a flying bomb. We had been so absorbed in the film, and the burning of Atlanta in the American Civil War, that we hadn't heard a thing.

Just before I left school, my father was made a Rear-Admiral, hoisting his flag in H.M.S. *Birmingham* for the final months of the war. It was the height of his ambition. He was to command the 10th Cruiser Squadron, as second in command of the Home Fleet.

We celebrated V.E. Day at St. Mary's with a huge party for the whole town, on our playing fields, and a bonfire on which we gleefully burnt effigies of Hitler and Mussolini – you can't fight a war without hating the enemy. At the end of the term I left school, with six months till I had to take up the place I had been offered at the Froebel College in London. I chose to stay at Ardoch with my mother, to help with the local Girl Guides, and to have the most wonderful piano lessons from the head of music at Glasgow University, A. M. Henderson. He taught me more about music in six months than I had learnt in six years at school. Perhaps it was thanks to his inspired teaching that I was able to take on the chairmanship of the Scottish Baroque Ensemble, with Leonard Friedman as its unique and talented Leader, much later in my life.

While I was Lieutenant of the Cardross Guide Company, we took them to camp on an estate near North Berwick – the *Birmingham* happened to be anchored in the Forth at the time, and my father invited all the Girl Guides on board his ship for tea. It was an experience they were never to forget, and the highlight of the week's camp!

My mother and I were at Ardoch when the news finally came through, after the horror of Hiroshima, that the war in the Far East was over, too. That night all the ships at the Tail of the Bank on the Clyde sounded off their ships' sirens, and rockets cascaded into the sky. Next day my mother and I joined rejoicing crowds in Glasgow, who crowded into George Square to celebrate. At one point I believe we had six sailors perched on the roof and bonnet of our car. It was a memorable night in the midst of that happy, thankful crowd. The war was over at last, and our family had survived more or less intact. But there were to be two tragic losses – my two eldest cousins, Nicholas Fitzherbert, and "Bil" Brooke, were both killed on active service. They had been my mother's two pages at her wedding in 1924.

Early in 1946 I made my "debut" at the Queen Charlotte's Ball in London. My own party of eight consisted of three school friends and myself, and four young Naval officers as our partners. Tragically, my cousin Nicholas was killed in a flying accident in the Fleet Air Arm the previous night, so much loved cousin, Bill (his brother), was unable to come to the party. As the war had only just ended we did not take part in a proper "season" that year, but I was invited to several dances and I was also invited with my parents to the first Garden Party at Buckingham Palace since the War, at which I was presented to Queen Elizabeth, to my great pride and delight.

A huge "V.J. Day" Parade was held later in the year, and my father flew his flag in H.M.S. *Diadem,* which was the guard ship for the parade, stationed in the Thames. He had several parties on board, and the night before the parade he was to have a special dinner-party for the First Lord of the Admiralty. Unfortunately my mother developed flu that day, so Fa told me that I would have to stand in for her on board the *Diadem* that night as hostess for his dinner-party. I was extremely nervous, but I was determined to do it properly. I suppose I must have managed, even though I was only just eighteen, because the First Lord of the Admiralty, Mr A. V. Alexander, invited me to come to Admiralty House next day, to watch the great Victory Parade from his balcony.

I was, of course, thrilled to the marrow. I arrived in good time, and suddenly felt very young and shy when I realised that all his other guests were admirals, with their wives. I found myself standing beside a very friendly looking admiral when we were given a glass of champagne on arrival, so I decided to ask him if he knew my father. Of course he did, and he told me that he was The Mackintosh of Mackintosh. I had not only found a kind admiral to look after me, but he came from Scotland as well, it was too good to be true!

And so my childhood as a sailor's daughter came to an end standing on the balcony at Admiralty House, in sight of Nelson on his column in Trafalgar Square. It was the unbelievably happy ending to a nautical fairy tale. There had been good fairies and bad fairies in my story, but best of all, I had been whisked round the world on a magic carpet, and my experiences would fill a book. They just have!

THE END

# INDEX